Old Homes of South Carolina

Old Homes of South Carolina

Drawings and Text by Joy Stagg Rust

PELICAN PUBLISHING COMPANY
Gretna 1992

To my husband, Ray,
for loving encouragement
and valuable assistance

The word "Pelican" and the depiction of a pelican are
trademarks of Pelican Publishing Company, Inc., and are
registered in the U.S. Patent and Trademark Office.

Library of Congress Cataloging-in-Publication Data

Rust, Joy Stagg.
    Old homes of South Carolina / drawings and text by Joy Stagg
Rust.
        p.   cm.
    Includes index.
    ISBN 0-88289—874-4
    1. Architecture, Domestic—South Carolina—Guidebooks.
2. Dwellings—South Carolina—History.   I. Title.
NA7235.s6R8   1992
728′.37′09757—dc20   92-15746
                                                                    CIP

Manufactured in the United States of America

Published by Pelican Publishing Company, Inc.
1101 Monroe Street, Gretna, Louisiana 70053

CONTENTS

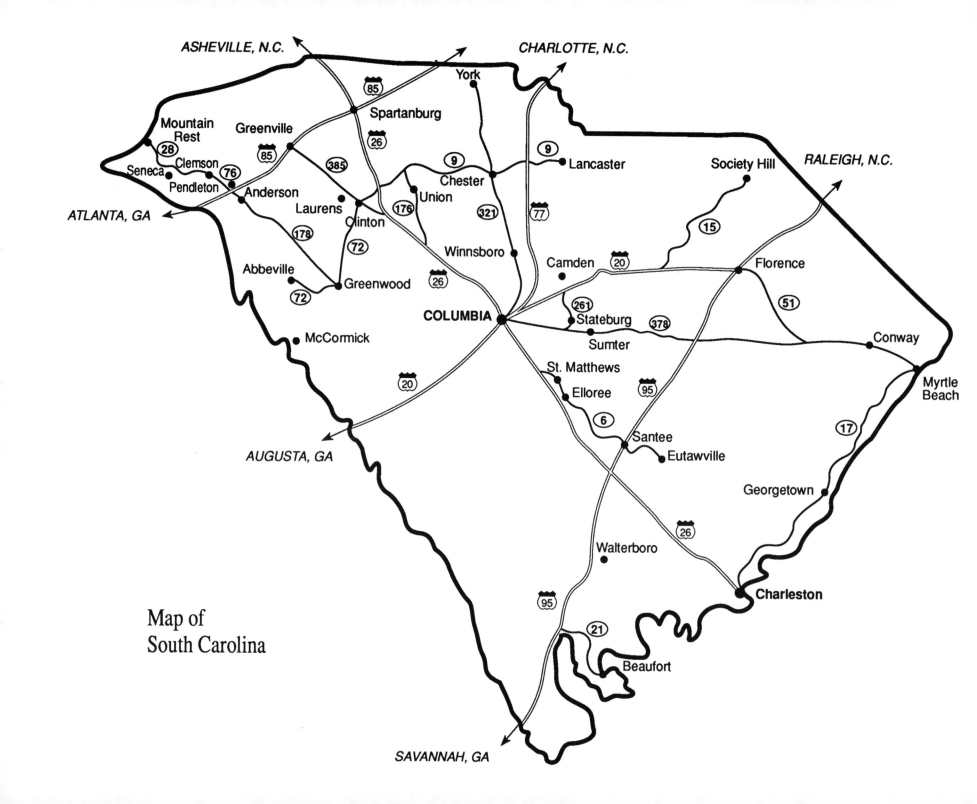

Map of
South Carolina

ACKNOWLEDGMENTS

Beaufort Historic Foundation
Charleston Historic Foundation
Camden Archives and Museum
Conway Library
Pendleton Historic Foundation
Sumter County Museum
Spartanburg Historic Society
State Department of Archives and History, Columbia, S.C.
Dr. and Mrs. Posey Belcher, Walterboro, S.C.
Mrs. Joe Cathcard, Winnsboro, S.C.
Anna P. Collins, Chester, S.C.
Mrs. Robert Cooper, Laurens, S.C.
Nell Morris Crible, Georgetown, S.C.
Dr. and Mrs. Robert Cuttino, Beaufort, S.C.
Dr. Russell Dean, Clinton, S.C.
Ginny Dubose, Sumter, S.C.
Jan Duke, Lancaster, S.C.
Dr. William Harris, Greenwood, S.C.
Rev. and Mrs. J. M. Kirkland, Georgetown, S.C.
Sharon Kuzbury, Camden, S.C.
Mrs. A. McCuen, Greenville, S.C.
Mrs. Jo McGee, Spartanburg, S.C.
Mrs. Evelyn Meador Miller, Columbia, S.C.
Ann Morris, Society Hill, S.C.
Mrs. Charles Moxley, Mountain Rest, S.C.
Rev. Horace Sims, Greenwood, S.C.
Mrs. B. J. Taylor, Anderson, S.C.

Special thanks go to Mrs. Brenda Jeffcoat of Columbia, S.C., for her help with proofreading, computer printing, etc.

THE BEGINNINGS

Charleston

In 1670 the Carolina proprietors sent out an expedition under William Sayle to settle the southern part of their holdings. Eight lords proprietors had been granted the territory south of Virginia and north of Florida with the authority to rule as they saw fit. They sought to establish a feudal state, but they made little headway with such plans. The grant was known as Carolana and later as Carolina. As early as 1654 settlers from Virginia migrated to Albemarle Sound, and this area became known as North Carolina toward the end of the seventeenth century.

The group with Sayle settled on the west bank of the Ashley River. They carried with them an eighteen-month supply of food, clothing, equipment for farming and building, as well as gifts for the Indians.

They built a fort and soon began planting. Early dwellings were very small and were probably built of small tree trunks sealed with mud or clay. By 1680 there were probably one thousand colonists living in Charles Town and on small farms along the Ashley and Cooper rivers. The settlement had been moved to a peninsula which was on higher ground, and the proprietors gave detailed instructions for the building of homes in this new location.

This new settlement quickly became a cosmopolitan town: immigrants from Ireland, the West Indies, Barbados, and New England began to arrive. As early as 1687 French Huguenots, fleeing from France to avoid religious persecution, were settling in Charles Town after a brief stay in Port Royal. In 1696 an entire congregation of twenty-eight Baptists left Kittery, Maine with their pastor, William Screven. They established a church in Charles Town which had originally been established in 1682 in Kittery. They left Maine in quest of religious freedom. Charles Town became a place noted for religious freedom with English, French, Quakers, Anabaptists, Baptists, and independent churches worshipping side by side.

Houses were built much like ships. Many of the early contractors were shipbuilders, and they used the same type of construction as that employed in their trade. Walls were constructed of logs, and gaps between these timbers were filled with straw, clay, and shells. Then they were often covered with plaster. The first colonists brought bricks with them to build chimneys, but they were soon making their own bricks with which they built entire homes. By 1713 all new homes were required to be of brick. Soon the homes became elegant dwellings with imported marble or carved mantels. Plans for the homes were obtained from London pattern books, but Dutch, Swedish, and German architecture also influenced the builders.

Cultivation of rice was introduced in the late years of the seventeenth century. The harbor of Charles Town brought in trade from the outside world. With all this activity, Charles Town enjoyed a lively social life not found in other places. It had become the resort city for South Carolina planters. Southern planters were very generous in their hospitality. There was constant visiting back and forth. The homes became larger to accommodate overnight guests.

The following pages present just a few of the many beautiful homes of that era which have survived the ravages of the passing years and fierce coastal storms. Some are open to the public and some are not except for annual tours. For more information write to: Historic Charleston Foundation, 51 Meeting Street, Charleston, S.C. 29401.

POSTMASTER BACOT HOUSE

54 Tradd Street

Tradd Street was named for Richard Tradd, who lived near here in 1670. Most of the streets on the peninsula were named for residents of the area. Some of the oldest houses in Charleston are located on this street. Among those is the Postmaster Bacot House, having been built in 1740.

This is one of the best examples of the Charleston single house. The single houses appeared in 1730 and are notable for narrowness and adaptability. They may be seen throughout the city of Charleston. Some are built on high arcaded basements and some on the ground. Some are made of brick and others of wood or stucco. Most are two-story structures, but many are three. There are two rooms to each floor bisected by a hallway with windows across from each other. This provided cool breezes of cross ventilation. The ceilings are high.

The only features that have been added to this house are the balconies by Susan Pringle Frost. These were salvaged from a building on State Street and are probably prerevolutionary. In many such homes a place of business would originally be located on the first level at the front with the entrance directly from the street. In those cases the family lived on the upper levels. This is the original arrangement for this house. Peter Bacot, having been appointed postmaster by George Washington, maintained his office at the front of the house and his residence was on the upper levels. A side entrance led to the stair hall and to the family residence.

On August 31, 1886 at 9:15 A.M. the entire area was shaken by a strong earthquake, and homes were damaged. Some of them were severely damaged with bricks broken. Earthquake rods were run through the houses to strengthen the old walls, and where bricks were badly broken the walls were covered with stucco. On some walls the stucco was scored to resemble stone. Note the earthquake bolts on these houses. The Postmaster Bacot House was finished in stucco to cover the earthquake damage.

This is a private home.

DR. WILLIAM
CLELAND HOUSE

60 Tradd Street

The single house pictured here is in the Georgian style and was built without a piazza. Originally, many of the houses were constructed without porches, which were added later. The house, built of brick and covered with stucco, is situated sideways on the lot with the gabled end facing the street. Note the earthquake bolts on the front and sides of the home. Apparently, George Ducot, a shipwright, built the house for his daughter, Margaret, occasioned by her second marriage in 1732 to Dr. William Cleland of Crail, Scotland.

This single of Tradd Street is one of the few within the original fortified city which escaped the disastrous fires of the seventeenth and eighteenth centuries. Tradd Street contains a notable group of early houses. That this house stands today is quite remarkable in view of the fact that very few houses survived the fires of 1698, 1699, 1700, 1731, and the latest of 1740.

This is a private residence.

JUDGE ROBERT PRINGLE HOUSE

70 Tradd Street

The builder of this lovely single house was a merchant of Charleston and a provincial judge who helped to open the revolution by resisting the Stamp Act. His residence is situated on what were lots eighty-seven and eighty-eight of the Grand Model of 1672. The house is remarkable for its fine proportions and beautiful decorations. In addition to Judge Pringle's family the house has a long history of connections with only two other families.

Many of the houses in Charleston have porches on the side called *piazzas*, and the Pringle House is a fine example. These piazzas are usually on the east or south sides of the houses. At first these were built in very simple style, designed to keep the hot sun from shining in the windows. In time, however, they became very elaborate with grillwork and woodwork. There are walls which separate the piazzas from the street. Upon entering the door there is a pleasant surprise in the view of the lovely garden on one side of the piazza and the house on the other. The entrance to the house is from the piazza.

The houses are situated sideways with the gabled end facing the street. Outbuildings are located beyond the houses on the narrow and deep lots.

Many of the older homes that survived the earthquake were built of brick as was this house. The cracks were large between the bricks and were covered with stucco at a later date.

The home is a private dwelling and only occasionally open to tours.

HEYWARD HOUSE

78-79 Church Street

Dubose Heyward lived in the smaller house on the right when he read of the real life story of Sammy Smalls and conceived the original idea of *Porgy and Bess*. George Washington addressed the city from a balcony which in earlier days was a part of the house on the left. These two homes have been combined for one dwelling.

The home is private.

WILLIAMS-CALHOUN MANSION

16 Meeting Street

Charles Walton Williams, a prominent banker and businessman, bought the property where this mansion stands during the War Between the States. Subsequently, he sold the lot but regained it in 1873. The house was built from 1876 to 1878. It has thirty-five rooms and 24,000 square feet of floor space. This structure is considered one of the most important Victorian homes in the East.

Built with small red bricks, it has three and one-half stories. There are blue-green slate quions at the corners (hard stones used to enforce an exterior corner or edge of a wall). Piazzas on the first and second floors on the south side are supported by Corinthian columns. The three-storied bay at the front is topped by a heavily ornamented pediment. The bays also have Corinthian columns and are flanked on each side by double windows crowned with a single arch.

Patrick Calhoun, son-in-law of Williams, inherited the property. He was the grandson of John C. Calhoun, vice-president of the United States. In 1934 the mansion was sold by R. S. Marigault to Vera McClure Findlay of Washington, D.C. for $25,000. It later belonged to Hollis Ayers. In 1976 Gedney M. Howe III acquired it and began restoration. It is currently operated as a house museum.

LADSON-POPPENHEIM HOUSE

31 Meeting Street

To see the sun sparkling on this beautiful white frame house is truly a treat. It sits back from the street in a lovely Georgian-designed garden with many camellias, crepe myrtle trees, sago palms, and other Charleston favorites. The fact that it is set back from the street is unusual since most of the houses on this peninsula are built right up to the sidewalks with the door to the piazza opening directly onto the sidewalk.

The home was built in 1792 by Gov. James Ladson, a member of a wealthy family of plantation owners. It is a typical Charleston single house with its entrance door originally leading into a hall that extends the length of the building. The front entrance now opens onto a piazza on the garden side.

Although there have been many changes in the interior of the house, some of the original woodwork remains. After Ladson died, the property was sold to Jeremiah Yates, whose brother owned the house at 27 Meeting Street. There are some similarities between one of the mantels on the second floor and one in the house at 27 Meeting Street.

Charles Furman owned the house from 1832 until 1844, when it was acquired by Erastus Beach. He added the piazzas on the garden side and added the empire parapet roof line that exists today. He also added the wrought-iron fence, rearranged the entrance hall, and changed the front door to a revival-style door. Black marble mantels were also installed.

This was one of the first Charleston houses to install gaslight and later to be wired for electricity.

In 1877 Christopher P. Poppenheim became the owner of the house. He added the two-story bay fronting on Meeting Street and a dining room. Poppenheim owned a rice plantation on the Cooper River and a hardware business on King Street.

The 1886 earthquake caused some serious damage, leaving cracks in the plaster in several rooms. The Charleston tornado of 1938 also heavily damaged the home.

The Poppenheim family was a very influential family in Charleston and was very active in civic affairs. Their love of the past practically made their home a museum. They were responsible for the planting of many of the lovely trees and shrubs. The garden featured a fountain with the figure of Narcissus, reputed to be a copy of one in the Kaiserhof Gardens in Germany.

Contact Historic Charleston Foundation about possible tours of this private home.

WILLIAM BULL HOUSE

35 Meeting Street

Stephen Bull established a plantation, Ashley Hall, on the Ashley River about 1670. In 1696 he was granted the lots at this address. The house, one of the oldest in Charleston, was built about 1720 by William Bull, son of Stephen.

The home at 35 Meeting Street is three and one-half stories and built of stucco on a high foundation. There are three bays facing Meeting Street and adorned with corner quioning and keystones. The doorway has a Federal-style pediment, and a fanlight projects from the hip roof. The double stone staircase entry probably dates from about 1800. The double piazzas on the south side are detailed in such a way as to indicate that they were added prior to 1840. The Meeting Street facade has remained virtually unchanged, but the interior has been altered through the years. In the early nineteenth century, Adamesque alterations were made to the mantlepieces and cornices in the principal rooms on the first two floors. The staircase also dates to the nineteenth century.

The first lieutenant governor of the Royal Colony of South Carolina was William Bull. William Bull II also served as lieutenant governor of the colony. In succession he owned and occupied the house on Meeting Street. William Bull II has the distinction of being the first native South Carolinian to receive a medical degree. He was educated at the University of Leyden.

Tradition says that this house was nearly identical to the Ashley Hall plantation home. The Bull House was later owned by the Hayne family, and then in 1895 it passed to Henry H. Ficken.

Gov. Robert Y. Hayne is said to have stood on the steps and dissuaded a group of nullificationists from going to the Battery, where they planned to seize a ship and declare war on the Union.

The Preservation Society of Charleston's Award of Noteworthy Preservation was awarded to this home in 1967. The residence is rated "Excellent" in the city Feiss Wright Survey of Charleston and is considered a "high contributary" to lower Meeting Street.

The house is private but opened often on the annual Meeting Street tours.

BRUNCH-HALL HOUSE

36 Meeting Street

According to some historians, the houses of the mid-1700s were taxed in direct relation to the number of feet of their frontage on a street. This finely proportioned 1740 Georgian frame house is a single house, one room wide with side piazzas.

The beautiful woodwork has been preserved through the years and features the original cypress paneling in the drawing room. The hinges on the doors carry the maker's initials, *L. H.* Even the original floors are intact. In the drawing room there is a Thomas Elfe mantel. It is the work of the renowned Charleston cabinetmaker.

Furniture in the drawing room is a mixture of French and English. The secretary is an eighteenth-century American Chippendale. The harpsichord is a reproduction of an eighteenth-century French instrument that is housed at Yale University. When you visit, the current owner will graciously and skillfully play the harpsichord on request.

The dining room contains an eighteenth-century English breakfast table that opens to seat ten people. The china cabinet is also eighteenth-century English. The chandelier is French. The original house extended no farther than the dining room; the 1860 addition included the hall and library. This home was a "one-carriage home," and the horse was kept in the city stable.

Originally, the "kitchen house," also built in 1740, was not attached to the main house. It was considered a fire hazard. The "cooking" fireplace and warming and baking ovens remain in their original state and are among the best preserved in the city. Currently the kitchen house is used as a bed and breakfast unit. Above the kitchen there is a sitting room, small kitchen, bedroom, and bath. Downstairs there is another sitting room, and the bedroom is in the original kitchen. The floors are original. The owners are delightful hosts who provide a generous breakfast in the small kitchen of each bed and breakfast unit.

It is not known just who it was that erected the first Christmas tree in Charleston, but there is a record as early as 1781 of the use of greenery to decorate during the season. The British had captured Charleston, and some of the Hessian officers were stationed at 36 Meeting Street. That Christmas they decorated with pine and cedar, but the records do not mention a tree inside the house.

NATHANIEL RUSSELL HOUSE

51 Meeting Street

The Nathaniel Russell house, built in 1808 by a native of Rhode Island, is not the "typical" Charleston house. There are no piazzas or porches. The entry is from the street.

Russell came to Charleston about 1765 to start an import-export business. His father was involved in the same business in Rhode Island, but later became the chief justice of that colony. Russell built a wharf and warehouse on East Bay Street with a home and office across the street. When he built the home at 51 Meeting Street, he was seventy years of age.

The three-story house is of red brick with bright-red brick trim. It is a study in curves and ovals. The middle floor is the principal one and has arches above the recessed windows. The narrow balcony has curves at each end and wraps around the corner in a curve. Windows extend to the floor and may be opened onto the balcony allowing the residents to take advantage of every breeze. The wing to the left of the house is oval and provides a view of the garden.

Guests are welcomed into the stair hall through a large, formal entry room. One of the most beautiful "flying staircases" to be seen anywhere seems to float from the first floor to the third. Cast plaster and carved wood are used throughout the house. The oval rooms are a favorite Adam device.

The designer of the house is unknown, but many think that it was a New England architect who designed many other beautiful homes in Charleston during this period.

The house is open to the public and is operated by the Historic Charleston Foundation.

POYAS-MORDECAI HOUSE

69 Meeting Street

Dr. Jean Ernest Poyas built this classic Charleston single house in 1788. It is built in the elegant Adamesque style of architecture. This house is a three-and-one-half-story stuccoed brick structure on a high basement. The piazzas on the first and second levels are supported by Doric columns. Notice the dentil molding on the second level and at the top of the main house. The entry is through the piazza. The door is flanked by Ionic columns supporting the pediment above the door.

The most interesting feature of this stately mansion is the treatment of the windows. Each level is different. The first level has an arched treatment above the windows, the second has a triangular pediment, and the third floor windows have straight cornices above them.

Moses Mordecai purchased the house in 1837. The current owners have recently restored the structure. This home has been on the tour of Meeting Street during the Festival of Houses and Gardens sponsored by the Historic Charleston Foundation, which may be contacted for information concerning possible future tours.

EDMONSTON-ALSTON HOUSE

21 East Battery

One of the most beautiful houses in Charleston is located at 21 East Battery. It was built in 1829 by a Scottish immigrant, a Mr. Edmonston, who bought a wharf site and made a fortune in shipping, only to lose it all—including his house.

William Alston, a very wealthy planter from Georgetown, bought the property in 1839 and gave it to his son, Charles, who owned several rice plantations and a lovely home in Georgetown. George Washington visited Georgetown in 1791 and was a guest in Charles' home. Charles changed the appearance of the house on Battery Street from Federal to Greek Revival. He rebuilt piazzas with Doric columns on the first and second levels while using Ionic columns on the third. The hip roof was hidden behind a parapet. The house is stucco with stone quions at the corners. Beautiful wrought iron encircles the balcony on the middle level with the windows extending to the floor. There are two sashes in these windows with each one having six panes. When open the windows would catch the breezes. The middle floor is the principal area and is the location of the drawing rooms.

In later years, J. J. Pringle Smith, owner of Middleton Place Gardens, owned the house. It was inherited by his grandson, Charles H. P. Duell. The house is open to the public and is operated by the Historic Charleston Foundation.

MIDDLETON PLACE AND GARDENS

Ashley River Road (Highway 61)

The gardens of Middleton Place are America's oldest landscaped gardens. They were laid out in 1741 by Henry Middleton, the president of the First Continental Congress. His son Henry, governor of South Carolina and minister to Russia, introduced the lovely camellias which bloom in the winter and through the spring. Another son, William, planted the first azaleas. The gardens were ten years in developing with 100 slaves working on a daily basis.

Henry Middleton's son, Arthur, was one of the signers of the Declaration of Independence.

The original home was looted and burned by the Federal forces in 1865 during the War Between the States. The present home was built in 1755 as a guest wing. Almost all the furniture currently on display in the house belonged to the Middleton family. There are family portraits by Benjamin West and Thomas Sully. After the war, almost an entire set of Bourbon Spring china was found buried in the back of the stable yard. The chest at the foot of the bed in the winter bedroom was also found buried in the stable yard. Throughout this brick home are beautiful pieces of art, furniture, and china.

Henry Middleton owned twenty plantations, 50,000 acres of land, and 800 slaves. The original house was built sometime between 1704 and 1741. The two dependencies were added in 1741. Middleton Place was one of the most famous plantations along the river.

The entrance to Middleton Place is through the gardens. The plantation stable yards may also be visited. The restaurant located on the grounds serves Southern specialties, and interesting books and gifts are for sale in the gift shop. The home is now a house museum and is open daily with an admission charge.

DRAYTON HALL

Ashley River Road (Highway 61)

When the Federal troops approached Drayton Hall in 1865 there was a sign indicating the presence of the dread disease smallpox. The troops continued on their way and Drayton Hall was the only plantation home on the Ashley River Road that was not burned. It remains as a witness to the gracious living of the people of this area in earlier years.

Drayton Hall was built between 1738 and 1742. It was probably the first truly Palladian house in America and is one of the finest remaining examples of colonial architecture. John Drayton purchased land next to Magnolia, his father's plantation, and this was to be the center of his plantation.

The architect and builder of Drayton Hall are not known. The style is really a mixture of Georgian and Palladian. The land side of the red brick home has a two-story portico and may be the first of its kind in America. The house is built over a raised basement and has a double stairway both on the land front and the river front. The door on the river front has a pediment as do the three central windows on the upper level. The windows on the sides of the house have arches above them. The brick work seems to be the Flemish cross bond. Bricks form a flat arch over the remaining windows on each of the fronts.

Seven generations of Draytons have maintained the house in virtually its original condition. It has been painted only when it was built and again in 1870. It does not have electrical power, running water, or central heat. All of the rooms are paneled in cypress and the floors are pine. The moldings and the overmantels are beautifully carved.

Drayton Hall is an accredited museum with educational opportunities. There is a museum shop on the grounds. This home is now owned by the National Trust for Historic Preservation and the state of South Carolina. It is open to the public on a daily basis with tours on the hour beginning at 10:00. It is closed Thanksgiving, Christmas, and New Year's Day.

For additional information call (803) 766-0188.

THE LOW COUNTRY

Beaufort

Visit the city of Beaufort for a few days and you will want to return time and time again to amble along the tree-lined streets in the Historic District. Each house is truly a "gem" to be discovered by the interested viewer. The entire district is listed in the National Historic Register.

The history of Beaufort dates back to 1521, when Spanish named the city Punta de Santa Elena. The French Huguenots, led by Juan Ribault, first landed in the area called Port Royal in 1562 and stayed just a short time. The first English settlers landed in Beaufort and settled briefly before going on to establish a colony in Charles Town.

In 1710 the town was laid out and was named for Henry, the Duke of Beaufort. He was one of the lords proprietors who actually ruled much of South Carolina. Planters from Barbados were prominent among those who settled there. The influence of Barbados is seen in the architecture of many homes.

The style of architecture in Beaufort is different from that in other places throughout the state. While there is a close relationship to that of Charleston and Savannah, there is a definite difference. Most of the houses are of a frame, two-story, raised construction and painted white. They feature porticos across the front and some that wrap around the side. The roof of the portico or piazza is usually flat, and the house has a hip roof with gables on the ends. Some of these may have been built in the Federalist style with the piazzas added later. Usually, there was a central hall with an open stairway. A Palladian-type window was located at the landing.

Tabby construction utilized a concrete-type substance made of oyster shells and lime. This rough surface was covered with stucco on the outside and plaster on the inside. This is very durable construction featuring walls sometimes as much as fifteen inches thick. It provides a very comfortable interior.

The plaster and woodwork on the ceilings, cornices, and mantels in both types of homes are very lovely and of excellent quality. The mantels are usually in the Adam style. To see very ornate and exceptionally detailed work visit the Baptist Church, Beaufort.

Cruise ships and yachts sailing from the northeast coast to Florida and the Virgin Islands regularly schedule a stopover in Beaufort. The welcome center at the landing is well prepared for visitors. Horse-drawn carriages are available for touring. Throughout the year visitors are seen strolling along the streets of this historic city, and residents in the Historic District are very cordial. Bed and breakfast inns are operating in some of the most beautiful of the fine, old homes. A listing may be obtained from the visitor's center.

THE LEWIS REEVE
SAMS HOUSE

601 Bay Street

A splendid view of this house is afforded as one crosses the bridge over the bay. Apparently built by Lewis Reeve Sams in 1852, this home is a typical Beaufort structure. It is white frame on a raised basement with two-story verandahs across the front and a paneled balustrade that covers the roof line. The cornices on both levels are ornately denticulated. The fluted columns are Ionic on the second floor level and Doric on the lower. White marble steps lead to the front entrance. The door has sidelights and a transom with a pediment above that extends to the ceiling. The facings on the door are carved to reflect the fluted columns. The upstairs door corresponds to that of the main entrance. Windows are six over six flanked by shutters. Exterior and interior woodwork as well as the plaster work are superb. Mantels are of black marble.

During the War Between the States, the Union Army used the house for a hospital. After the war, the sons of Lewis Reeve Sams were able to recover their home, and in 1869 they sold it to a New Englander by the name of George Waterhouse, who had opened a general store in Beaufort during 1864.

The Lewis Reeve Sams House is now a bed and breakfast inn.

JOHN MARK VERDIER HOUSE

801 Bay Street

Beaufort was a prosperous town in the late 1700s. During that period five large houses were built using the same design. Three of those remain in very good condition. These are the Thomas Fuller House, the Elizabeth Barnwell Gough House, and the John Mark Verdier House. These are two-story houses on raised basements; the Verdier House is white frame on a tabby basement. The houses are built in the Federal style and have two-story porticos. There is very elaborate molding under the eaves of the pediment above the second level. The four lower columns are slender, round, simplified Doric. The front entrance is reached by double steps on each side of the portico. Above the door is a fan-shaped light. The windows are nine over nine and are flanked by shutters. A lovely paneled parlor is at one side of the entrance hall, and the dining room is on the other side. The mantels in these two rooms are Adam style. The carving of the capitals and molding inside the house is very delicate. Some think that these may have been added at a later date.

This house was built about 1786 by John Mark Verdier when he was twenty-six years of age. He was destined to become a very successful merchant. The Marquis de Lafayette was one of the many influential guests in the home. He visited in 1825. The Union forces headquartered there during the War Between the States.

After the war this home was used for many purposes during which time it suffered substantial deterioration. Finally, it was condemned. A group of citizens determined that this structure would be saved. After many struggles, restoration began in 1955 and was completed in 1976. The Historic Beaufort Foundation owns the home and has offices in the basement. It is now a house museum and is open to the public. An admission is charged.

THE GEORGE ELLIOTT HOUSE

1001 Bay Street

Imagine this house without the second-story verandah—it must have been spectacular. Huge columns resting on square pillars extended to the roof without any obstruction. That is the way that George Elliott built this home in 1840. The well-designed iron railings on the lower level are most unusual for Beaufort. The second-floor verandah was probably added during the period between 1860 and 1880. At about that time Greek Revival porches were added to several homes. The railings on the upper level are turned wood matching the ones on the balustrade which covers the roof line. The front entrance door has sidelights and a fanlight with delicate carving above it. The upstairs door has double arched glass with a square transom above. Blinds flank the two-over-two windows.

Dr. W. A. Jenkins, one of the richest men in Beaufort, bought the house before the War Between the States. The fact that he owned 1,500 slaves reflects his wealth. Jenkins left behind valuable books and papers at the beginning of the war. Someone moved those possessions to Hilton Head, and they were recovered by Jenkins after hostilities had ceased. The Federal government sold the house for taxes, and George Holmes purchased it.

It is now a house museum and is open to the public.

JOHN CUTHBERT HOUSE

1203 Bay Street

"Surely, this house is out of a fairy tale" is the thought that comes to mind at the first sight of this sparkling white house with its "gingerbread" trim. The structure is perched on top of pale pink pillars. Built in 1811, the Cuthbert House is two-story white frame on a raised foundation. There is a double portico, and Tuscan columns support the pedimented roof. On both sides of the portico there is a one-story bay porch with highly decorated Victorian cornices. On the first floor there are two shuttered windows on each side of the front door. The front entrance has a semi-elliptical fanlight as well as sidelights. The upstairs door also has sidelights. The windows are four and four. The woodwork on the interior and exterior is outstanding. There are central hallways on both floors. In the late nineteenth-century, rooms, bay windows, Victorian trim, and the porches on each side were added.

John Alexander Cuthbert built this house for his bride, Mary B. Williamson. When they were married part of the dowery was a number of slaves which they received in 1811. At one time, Cuthbert was pastor of the First Baptist Church of Washington, D.C. He was the author of a biography of Thomas Fuller.

The Cuthbert House became the property of United States Army Brig. Gen. Rufus Saxton during the War Between the States. On one occasion General Saxton entertained General Sherman in his home. In 1862 Saxton was made director of Freedman Affairs and Cultivation. A part of his responsibility was to take possession of abandoned plantations. He was sympathetic with the freed slaves and hoped to make them independent citizens, but he had such difficulty in managing the plantations that he had to give up on his experiment. The government began to auction the plantations in 1863. General Saxton continued his efforts to protect the rights of the freedmen.

Recently restored, this house is a beauty to behold. It is privately owned.

THE THOMAS FULLER HOUSE (THE TABBY MANSE)

1211 Bay Street

The Tabby Manse, one of the oldest homes in Beaufort, has exterior walls made entirely of tabby. The walls are two feet thick and covered with a scored stucco. During this period there were five homes built in Beaufort with tabby walls or foundations. Only three remain. The designs of all the houses are similar and influenced subsequent architecture in Beaufort. The Tabby Manse still has its original eight rooms and has the same exterior except for an addition at the rear. The front has a double-tiered, pedimented portico over a high arcaded basement. With the basement being wider than the portico, a terrace is formed at each end. On the first floor behind the columns are four engaged wooden columns. Two large six over six windows with louvered blinds are on each side of the portico. The simple entrance is flanked by engaged columns.

Paneling and wainscoting in the rooms are of cypress and yellow heart pine. Three of the rooms are completely paneled. The mantels are Adam style. There is a central hall with a divided stairway; a Palladian window at the back lights the stairs.

The Tabby Manse was built by Thomas Fuller in 1786, which was the same year he married Elizabeth Middleton. Fuller was an outstanding planter. Their son, Richard, one of seven children, went to Harvard Law School and finished twentieth in his class. When Richard became a Christian, he gave his last "boisterous" party and invited all his old friends from his days when he partied in that manner. He made a speech declaring his faith in God and renouncing his old ways. He became a very well-known and highly respected Baptist minister. Under his leadership, the Baptist Church of Beaufort was built.

Rev. Mansfield French, an abolitionist Methodist minister, bought the house during the War Between the States.

For a number of years during the twentieth century, the Outbanks and the Greenwoods operated a guesthouse here. It became a favorite place of artists, writers, and architects.

This is a private home not open to visitors.

THE HENRY MCKEE HOUSE (ROBERT SMALL HOUSE)

511 Prince Street

The history of this house reveals a most interesting relationship not generally understood to be characteristic of the time of the War Between the States. Henry McKee built it in 1834. There were slave cabins behind it on the back of the lot. Robert Small was born a slave (1839) in one of the cabins. He had a comfortable life as he was growing up. His master hired him out in Charleston in 1851, and he lived there until the beginning of the War Between the States. Small became a pilot for ships and captured the ship known as *Planter*. He delivered this vessel to the Federal forces in Beaufort. For this heroic feat, he received considerable prize money. He also was involved in the war effort by guiding Union ships in their attacks on Sea Island. With his prize money he bought the Henry McKee house in 1863 at a tax sale. He and his descendants occupied the house for over eighty years until 1940.

The McKees had sold the home to the DeTrevilles in 1855. After the war they tried to regain the house through court action. The case was ultimately appealed to the Supreme Court and decided in Small's favor. This case provided validity for the acts of Congress between June 7, 1862 and February 6, 1863 providing for direct taxes on property in occupied territory and penalties for nonpayment. Small became a state legislator, United States congressman, and customs collector for the Port of Beaufort.

Small's character was revealed in the poignant story of his care for Mrs. McKee. The McKees moved back to Beaufort after the war and Mr. McKee died, leaving Mrs. McKee alone. One day when she was quite old, she wandered into the home where she had lived, thinking it still belonged to her. Small took her to her old room, and until her death, he and his family waited on her as though she were the mistress of the house.

This large frame house with a two-story portico originally had a one-story front porch. The change was made in 1870. The roof is supported by Doric columns and has a plain cornice. The plan is much like the typical Beaufort house with its central hall and two rooms on each side. There were three rooms across the back forming a *T*. All of the mantels are Adam style as is the main entrance on the first level with a transom added. The second floor door has sidelights. Upstairs windows are nine over nine, and those downstairs are six over six and flanked by plantation shutters.

This is a private home and not open to the public.

TIDALHOLM
(THE EDGAR FRIPP HOUSE)

1 Laurens Street

Two movies, *The Great Santini* (1979) and *The Big Chill* (1983), were filmed at Tidalholm. It is in one of the most picturesque areas of the city of Beaufort. The home, built in 1856 by Edgar Fripp, is located on the banks of the Beaufort River. The river is visible from three sides of the house. Fripp made his home on St. Helena Island; he built Tidalholm as a summer home to use as an escape from the mosquitos on the island. The white frame structure is of Italian style. Edgar's brother, James, owned the house during the War Between the States. When he returned following the war, the house was being sold to pay the taxes. Fripp did not have the money to bid on the house, so he stood by with tears streaming down his cheeks as his home was being sold. According to reports of the event, a Frenchman who bought the house walked over, and gave Fripp the keys, and immediately returned to France.

Square columns dominate the wraparound, two-level portico. The house is set high above the ground with handsome brick steps leading to the front entrance. The pedimented windows are flanked by shutters. A massive door with sidelights and transom light has a pediment that extends to the top of the wall. The door on the second floor has double arched panes. Attention is inevitably drawn to the beautiful molding on the porticos.

Tidalholm has been very influential in Beaufort culture. Many have visited this place and returned to make Beaufort their home. The house was restored in 1974. It is not open to the public.

THE OAKS
(PAUL HAMILTON HOUSE)

100 Laurens Street

Col. Paul Hamilton, grandson of Paul Hamilton who served as secretary of the Navy under President Madison, built this Italian-style house in 1856. The oaks which frame the house are massive with long, outstretched limbs. This white frame home is built on a raised foundation of brick. Wide porches wrap around the sides of the house. The columns on the upstairs porch are round Corinthian while those on the lower level are square with a Doric capital. Braces in pairs support the wide overhanging roof. The windows are unusual. They are wider than normal and also have sidelights. On the first floor the shutters are double. A straight, elaborate pediment tops the windows and the front door on this level. The pediment on the windows and door on the second level are arched.

When Beaufort was occupied in 1861 by Federal soldiers the house was deserted. It was auctioned in November of 1865. Colonel Hamilton went to Charleston to secure the money to buy his residence, but the auction took place before he could return. George Holmes, a Northern merchant, was visiting friends in Beaufort at the time of the auction and bought the house in Hamilton's name.

This home is not open to the public.

THE BERNERS BARNWELL SAMS HOUSE NO. 2

201 Laurens Street

The first house built by Dr. Berners Barnwell Sams stands on New Street and was built in 1818. During the War Between the States, the house was confiscated and used as a hospital for slaves. In 1852 Dr. Sams built the imposing mansion at 201 Laurens Street. The house is built of brown-beige plantation bricks on a raised foundation. There are four huge Doric pillars with a two-story portico. The balustrade on both levels is made of some type of metal that has been handsomely pierced. The windows have pale brown-toned shutters. The woodwork on the balustrade around the flat top roof of the portico is similar to that of the balustrades on the two levels of the verandah. Built of tabby, the original kitchen, blacksmith shop, carriage house, and laundry are separate from the house and are currently used as guest rooms.

It was used as a hospital during the War Between the States. This house was among the many houses that were sold to pay the taxes, and it was bought by William Wilson. Later it was used as the St. Helena rectory when Rev. A. P. Hay was the pastor. He was called "the poet of the Confederacy."

The house has been owned by the descendants of George Crofut since 1895. It is not open to the public.

MARSHLANDS

301 Pinckney Street

Facing the marshlands of the Beaufort River is the James Robert Verdier House. It is named Marshlands in recognition of the most prominent feature of the view from its one-story piazza, which wraps around the sides of the house. This piazza is supported by square columns and double stairs leading up to it. The stair bannister is trimmed in dark green, and the shutters are the same color. The house is built over a cellar which has pale pink tabby arches. This architecture of this two-story white frame house is typically Beaufort, but also of the Federal era with a West Indies or Barbados influence. The front entrance has sidelights and a fanlight and there are two windows on each side of it. The central window upstairs also has sidelights, providing light to the central stairs.

There is a gable in the middle of the red metal roof which has dentil molding. The roof cornice has the same molding.

This home was built for Dr. James Robert Verdier in about 1814. Verdier treated yellow fever with some success, and because of this was quite prominent in the area. The house was used as headquarters for the United States Sanitary Commission during the War Between the States. It is listed on the National Historic Register and is a private dwelling.

THE JOHN JOHNSON HOUSE
804 Pinckney Street

This large, three-story, classic revival house, one of the most stately homes in Beaufort, was built by Dr. John Johnson and his wife, Claudia Tailbird, in 1850. There are piazzas on the second and third levels on three sides with eight columns across the front. The columns downstairs are Doric, and those upstairs are very ornate Corinthian. The lower level has massive square pillars.

The house faces Hancock Street, but the entrance is on Pinckney. The door opening to the piazza on the Hancock Street side is very large with sidelights and a transom. Leading to the second level entry are marble steps with black wrought-iron bannisters. All of the mantels are also marble. The walls are eighteen inches thick and are of unusually large brick. This same type of brick is used in the construction of the four chimneys. The bricks have been painted white.

The John Johnson house is a private home.

ELIZABETH HEXT HOUSE (RIVERVIEW)

207 Hancock Street

The Hext House was built in about 1720 and is considered to be the second oldest in Beaufort. Elizabeth Hext was born in 1746, the only child of Francis Hext and his wife, Elizabeth Stanyarne. When she was fifteen years of age, she married William Sams of Wadmalaw Island. He bought Datha Island near Beaufort in 1783, and they raised their family there. When Elizabeth died she was buried on Datha Island beside her husband. The Hext House remained in their family until 1864.

Considered a small house by Beaufort standards, Riverview is a white frame house that has a high tabby foundation. There are upper and lower piazzas, each supported by six slender, round columns. The windows are six over nine, and much of the original glass remains. They are flanked by shutters. The front door has a transom light above it; chimneys stand at each end of the house. There are two rooms on each side of a center hall with two bedrooms upstairs. The gardens are quite spacious and well maintained. This is a private home.

ELIZABETH BARNWELL GOUGH HOUSE

705 Washington

A handsome brick and wrought iron wall and tall moss-draped trees frame the Elizabeth Barnwell Gough House. Elizabeth Barnwell was the granddaughter of John Tuscarona Barnwell, who built Fort King George on the Altamaha River. The fort was built in 1721 to provide protection for the colony from the advances of the Spanish. Richard Gough, Elizabeth's husband, served as a representative in the South Carolina General Assembly. Marianna, born in 1773, was their only child, and Richard and Elizabeth eventually separated after quarreling. Edward Barnhill built the house for Elizabeth with money left by her father for that purpose.

Marianna married James Smith, and they had ten children. Six of the boys changed their last name to Rhett, the name of their great-great-grandfather, Col. William Rhett. One of these sons, Robert Barnwell Rhett, was one of the strongest supporters of the nullification doctrine and the secessionist movement in South Carolina.

This was one of the five houses of tabby construction built in the 1700s (see Thomas Fuller House). Local builders adopted the Adam style using the materials at hand. This two-story structure rests upon an arcaded, raised basement, and the outside walls are tabby covered with stucco. Like the Fuller House, there is a two-tiered pedimented portico. The columns are slender Doric, and the ones on the upper level are smaller. There are simple stick-type balustrades enclosing both levels of the portico. The central entrance has pilasters on each side and a transom above with an Adam-style pediment over the door. There are two windows of six over six on each side of the door. A very simple doorway opens on the second-floor portico.

The floor plan of the house, very typical of Beaufort, was also used in the Fuller House and a number of others. The first floor has four rooms with a central hallway from front to rear and has a Palladian window lighting the double stairway. The heart pine and cypress paneled ballroom is located on the second floor. Two of the original mantels are still in place, and most of the woodwork on the second level is original.

This is a private dwelling.

SECESSION HOUSE
(MILTON MAXEY HOUSE)
1113 Craven Street

A tabby house was erected on this location in approximately 1724. The lot was later granted to Robert Williams in about 1743. When Milton Maxey went to Beaufort in 1800 he bought the property, removed the tabby second floor, and added two stories of wood construction. Maxey was from Massachusetts and went South to begin a school.

Edmund Rhett was the next owner of the house. Sometime after 1830 (maybe as late as 1860), Rhett practically destroyed all except the tabby basement and rebuilt two white frame levels on it. He also added a two-level Greek Revival porch supported by fluted Corinthian columns over fluted Ionic columns. Five arches extend over the pale pink basement. Curving marble steps lead to the entrance which is at one end rather than in the center of the porch. The doors on both levels have sidelights and transom lights. Woodwork around the doors is intricately carved as is the dentil molding on the upper and lower cornice.

The first ordinance of secession was drawn up in the east room of this house. The Beaufort County delegation gave full support to secession. The delegates left from this house to go to the boat landing and on into Charleston to cast their votes for secession from the Union. The property was taken over by the Union Army during the war and was used in several ways, one of which was as the headquarters for Gen. Rufus Saxton.

Georgetown

Georgetown history can be traced back to 1729 when Elisha Screven and William Swinton laid out the plan for the city. It was laid out in blocks with five streets running parallel to the Sampit River, and seventeen streets running perpendicular to the river. Although the size of the city has increased, this plan is still in effect. This entire area is on the National Historic Register. The city is the third oldest in the state and has been very important historically, agriculturally, and architecturally. It has also been important militarily. During the American Revolution, Georgetown was captured by the British on July 1, 1780 and recaptured by Gen. Francis Marion in 1781. On February 25, 1865, it was occupied by the Union naval forces, and the Winyah Indigo Society Building was used as a Union hospital.

The principal crops were indigo and rice. England put a bounty on indigo, and many planters became very wealthy. However, rice was the dominant crop, and at the peak of its culture in 1850, Georgetown was the largest exporter of rice in the world. When the planters lost their slaves there was not enough labor to be found to continue with rice farming. Then when the new heavy machinery was introduced, it was discovered that the land was too soft to support it.

Rice planters lived in large plantation homes outside of Georgetown. Many of these homes are still in excellent condition. The planters also had homes in Charleston where they went for extended visits. Their children were educated at home by tutors and then went abroad to continue their education.

Architecture ranged from simple colonial to elaborate plantation-style homes. The records do not reveal very much about the homes within the city itself.

Georgetown was named for King George II of England. The town was visited by George Washington in 1791. Other presidents visiting Georgetown were James Monroe, Martin Van Buren, Grover Cleveland, and possibly Franklin Delano Roosevelt.

Many interesting places may be seen touring this county. The women of the Prince George Winyah Parish sponsor an annual tour of the plantation homes. There are more than thirty homes in the Georgetown area that are on the National Register, and walking tours are available for the historic section of the city.

WITHERS-DALEY HOUSE

405 Front Street

Built in 1737, the Withers-Daley house is thought to have originally been a tavern. The floor plan of the home is different from others constructed about the same time. Other houses had a central hall with a single front entrance and rooms on each side of the hall. This one had a hall to the right with the rooms to the left, and it had two front doors.

About 1975 the home was restored, and in the basement a catacomb storage rack was found which added to the evidence that it had, indeed, been a tavern. The home was originally one room deep with porches all around it. The rear piazza was enclosed to create more rooms. The slanting front porch floor allowed water to drain away. The roof is gabled and has twin chimneys. Windows upstairs are six over six and downstairs they are nine over nine with dark shutters. Wooden pegs for hanging clothes can still be seen in the upstairs bathroom.

Vice-President Aaron Burr stayed overnight here on his way to Brookgreen Gardens.

This is a private home.

THE HAROLD KAMINSKI HOUSE

1003 Front Street

Beautiful moss-covered trees provide a perfect setting for this lovely home on the banks of the Sampit River. The home was probably built in 1760 by Benjamin Alston, the father of Governor Alston. By way of succession the home became the residence of Harold and Julia Pyatt Kaminski, Benjamin's great-great-granddaughter.

Heiman Kaminski was born in Prussia in 1839 and went to Charleston in the 1850s. Soon after, he went to Georgetown to work as a clerk in the mercantile house of E. Baum. Later he was transferred to Conway, and he was there at the outbreak of the War Between the States. He was one of the first to join Brooks Guards of the Confederate States of America. Kaminski founded Kaminski Hardware Company, and in early 1970 it was the oldest existing business in the county. In that year its location was changed for the first time. For 105 years the business was located in the Kaminski Building at 633 Front Street. Mr. Kaminski died in 1923 and Mrs. Kaminski willed the house to the city of Georgetown. It contains a priceless collection of antiques.

Six square Doric columns that extend the height of the verandah support the hip-type roof. Matching pilasters are at each end of the house. There is a small wrought-iron balcony on the second level. The balustrade is across the front with the steps at the end of the porch. The paneled front door has sidelights and a fanlight in the transom above it. The windows are framed by shutters.

This building is operated as a house museum.

PAWLEY HOUSE

1019 Front Street

The front of the Pawley House faces the river, but the rear of the house is equally as lovely in appearance. The wings on each side were added in about 1812. An inscription on a windowpane reads as follows: "J. W. Pawley 1815." The home was built in 1790 on a raised, arcaded basement with double curved steps leading to the main floor. Doric columns support the roof of the one-story verandah. The hip roof of the house has two dormers. Twin chimneys at each end of the structure rise high above the second-story roof line. Today, this building is the home office of First Federal Bank.

When George Washington visited Georgetown in 1791 he spent the night in this home and made a speech at the Masonic Lodge.

This elegant home is constructed of brick covered with stucco. The windows are nine over nine and flanked by louvered blinds.

HERIOT-TARBOX HOUSE

15 Cannon Street

A slight bluff overlooking the Sampit River provides the setting for the Heriot-Tarbox House. It fronts the river, and at the time it was built guests arrived by boat. The owner operated one of the largest docks in Georgetown on his property. The frame double house has four rooms on each floor with lovely interior woodwork. There is a high, raised, arcaded, brick basement. This was an unusual building feature designed as a stabilizer in the event of flooding. The basement area was cooler than the house above; milk, cheese, and eggs were probably stored there. The windows on the upper floor are set high. This provides at least one indicator supporting the date of construction as approximately 1740. The hip roof line is original, and the view of the river from the dormer is excellent. The one-story piazza with Doric columns wraps around from front to side. The balustrade has an intricate "stick" design.

This house is the setting for a legend featuring a young lady who was protected and shielded by her parents. One day a sailing ship pulled into the dock, and she met a young man who was employed on the vessel. A romance began to blossom. The parents had other plans for their daughter, and they were most unhappy about this turn of events. Finally, the father told the captain of the ship that he did not want him to stop at his dock anymore. The girl never married. According to the legend the girl assisted in the war effort by holding a lamp in the upstairs window to indicate to the blockade runners whether or not it was safe to enter the port. There are some who vow that she may still be seen in the upstairs window waiting for her beloved's ship to return.

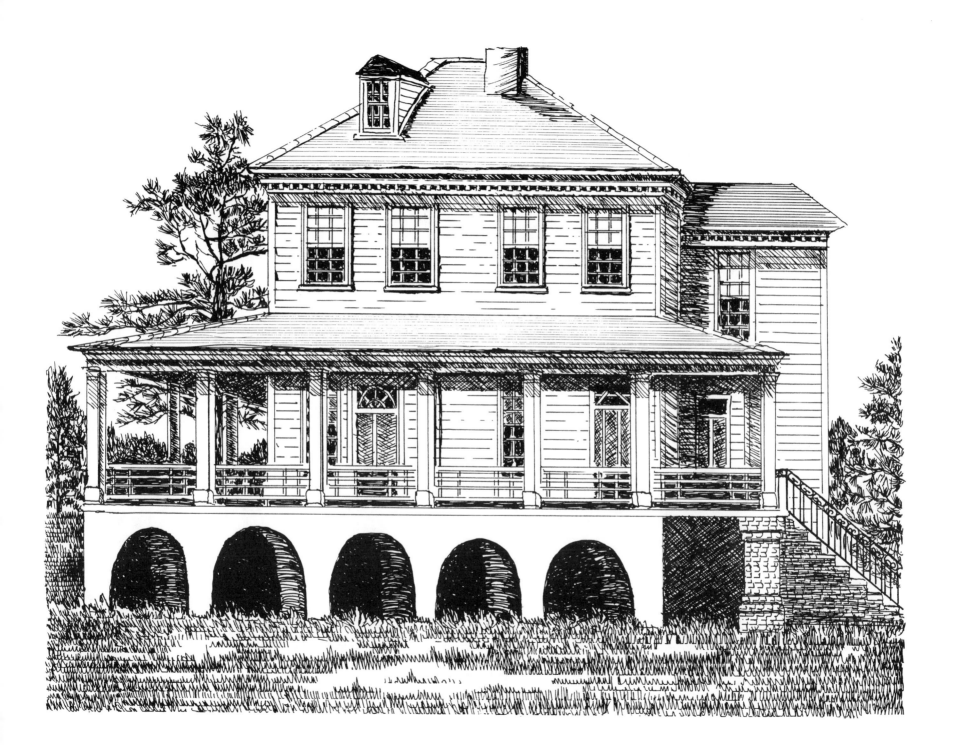

BOLLING-HENNING-STEARNS HOUSE

719 Prince Street

Mr. Bolling, the first owner of this house, was the person in Georgetown with authority to sign official papers and documents. Having been built in 1739, the house is the second oldest in the city. It is the only remaining house with double piazzas. They feature Doric columns that rest on brick posts on the first floor. The roof is tin with a gable, and there is a definite sway in the roof line. The frame house appears to sit right on the ground. Georgetown did not have sidewalks until the beginning of this century, and when they were laid the sidewalks went around the porch of this house. The original, random-width floors remain. One board may be three inches wide, and the next may be eight inches. Behind the living room is a sitting room, and the two are connected by a pocket door (a sliding door that disappears into the wall) which is still in good working order.

This is a private home.

RAINEY-CAMLIN HOUSE

909 Prince Street

Joseph H. Rainey was the first owner of this house built in 1760. He was the first black state legislator and the first of his race to serve as a United States congressman from South Carolina. Records reveal that he served ably in each post. How was a black man free in the South at that point in history? Rainey was a boiler by trade, and he had bought freedom for himself and his family. However, when the War Between the States began he found that the South was not the place to live. He moved to Barbados and remained until the conclusion of the war, at which time he returned to Georgetown. It was at this time that he ran for office and was elected.

The present owners have restored the home. In the process they discovered a decorative fireback (chimney back) made of heat-resistant material that fits at the back wall of the fireplace. Its purpose is to radiate heat into the room. Also discovered was stenciling which framed the bedroom windows. The original woodwork, floors, and windows remain in the house.

The house is frame with a one-story verandah. The hip roof has dormers and gables. Windows upstairs are nine over six, and on the first level they are nine over nine. All the windows are framed by shutters. The entrance steps are at one end of the porch. This is a private home.

PYATT-BROGDON HOUSE

630 Highmarket Street

There are only a few houses in Georgetown with arched foundations. The Pyatt-Brogdon House is one of those. Built in 1790, it sits on a very high basement. It is the only house in which Bermuda stone and coral rock are used for the foundation. This stone was brought into the city ports on sailing vessels. At one time the area under the house was open, and this is where the cooking was done. The servants may have lived here, also.

Double steps lead to the one-story verandah, which wraps around both sides of the home. The posts are modified Doric with a plain cornice. The cornice on the second level is denticulated. Three dormers protrude from the front of the hip roof. The central door has a sunburst light in the transom above it. There are two windows of nine over nine on each side of the door. On the second floor there are five windows. Instead of louvered blinds there are paneled shutters.

Much of the ornamentation such as the chair rail, wainscoting, and the outside bannisters is original. The home is now a bed and breakfast inn, with the owner residing on the highest level.

Walterboro

The town of Walterborough (the early spelling) was given its name by Paul and Jacob Walterborough. These brothers were low-country planters and built the first house in the area in 1783. Walterborough became a summer retreat for rice planters. By 1832 the summer population was about nine hundred; the winter population was considerably less. The town was made the seat of justice for the Colleton District in 1817, which ensured steady growth and development.

A number of the homes built in the nineteenth century have survived. There were two types. One of these was a gabled-roof, one-story house raised on brick pillars with a central hall and verandah. The other was a two-story house with a similar plan. Some had two-story verandahs and others just the one tier. The Greek Revival, Colonial Revival, and decorated cottages followed. There are huge, beautiful, moss-draped oak trees throughout the historic district. Walterboro is thirty-two miles inland from the Atlantic Ocean.

GLOVER-MCLEOD HOUSE
109 Savage Street

Walter J. McLeod, an attorney, and his wife have lived in this spacious, tree-shaded house since 1938. The home was built in 1835 for Mr. H. C. Glover. After only four years, Glover sold the property to Major Worley of the Antwerp Plantation. This was to be used as a summer home. The McLeods purchased it from the Hamacks family.

The white frame house is built on what is probably the highest elevation in Walterboro. There is a two-story verandah, and the first level wraps around one side of the home. Beautiful turned columns with a plain cornice support the shed roof. The balusters which circle the piazzas are turned to match the columns. The downstairs windows are quite unusual. On either end there are tall windows that are two over two. The windows on each side of the front entrance are not the same height as the ones on the ends, and each has a transom light above it. They are also two over two. All the windows on both floors have rounded pediments and are flanked by dark shutters. The front entrance has sidelights, a transom, and the rounded pediment. The gardens around the home are quite lovely. A red-brick walk and brick steps lead to the raised house. Red-brick chimneys rise above each end of the gabled roof.

This is a privately owned home.

DENT-LINING-MCDANIEL-HIOTT HOUSE

418 Wichman Street

Documents related to this house do not identify the builder, but the front part of the house was built before 1838. Elizabeth A. H. Dent, the widow of the commander of the frigate *Constitution (Old Ironsides)*, became the owner in 1841. Later the Dents' son-in-law, Thomas Lining, was the owner, and from him the McDaniel family acquired the property. Dr. and Mrs. David Hiott were subsequent owners.

Apparently, there have been a number of additions and changes through the years. Originally the home was one story. The front hall and two large rooms on the front have hand-hewn timbers and pegged construction. In 1861, Lining was the owner. At that time the back halls, four back rooms, and the kitchen were added. Sometime during the ownership of the McDaniel family a second floor was added. At the present this white frame home has two floors with a hip roof. A two-story curved porch at the center of the front has four very large Ionic columns supporting a curved cornice. At each side of this is a one-story flat-roofed porch with slender Doric columns. The front entrance to this very elegant house has sidelights and a fanlight.

This property is privately owned.

HENDERSON HOUSE (ORANGE GROVE)

Wichman Street

The sun shining through the towering trees creates lacy patterns on the seamed, red, tin roof and sparkling white clapboards of this lovely old home. Sitting on a red-brick foundation, this two-story house is fronted by a one-story verandah which wraps around each end. Doric columns support the shed-type roof. Brick steps with a wrought-iron handrail welcome one to the front entrance. The door has sidelights, and above it there is a fanlight. The woodwork around the door is well detailed.

Colonel Elmore built the Alex Henderson home in 1820. Subsequent owners were Daniel Henderson, Sallie and Charlotte Henderson, and Alice Neyle Henderson Jervey. At one time Jervey had an art studio called the "Orange Grove Studio."

Across the street from the Dent-Lining-McDaniel-Hiott House (418 Wichman Street) is a driveway that leads to the Henderson House. It is a private home.

PAUL-MCTEER-WICHMAN HOUSE

Paul Street

Huge moss-draped trees line the drive to this beautifully detailed home. The wood trim on the white frame house is elegant. Modified Doric paneled columns support the finely detailed triangular pediment of the front porch. There are matching engaged columns. The front entry is massive with sidelights, transom, and pilasters that mirror the four columns of the porch. The home is one story, but because of its height it imparts a sense of awe to anyone approaching the structure. The ceilings are fifteen feet high, and the windows are four feet by twelve feet. The closed black shutters contribute to the hushed appearance of the house.

Jonathon Lucas, an architect, built this home for James Lawrence Paul in 1847. There have been very few changes. Paul's brother, Sampson, purchased it when his brother left Walterboro in 1851. The following owner was L. S. McTeer, whose two daughters inherited his property at his death. One of his daughters, Jennie, was married to Albert Wichman, and she eventually became the sole owner of the house.

The very beautiful home has recently been repainted. It is located across the street from the funeral home on Paul Street, and is privately owned.

Eutawville

Eutawville is in the area referred to as the Santee River System. This area was settled very slowly because rice, the principal crop at that time, did not grow well. The invention of Whitney's gin in 1792, however, changed the circumstances. Cotton was a good crop for this region and the opening of the Santee Canal gave access to the Charleston markets.

There was heavy fighting in this vicinity during the Revolutionary War because Francis Marion ("The Swamp Fox") and General Moultrie both had homes here. Also, the Nelson Ferry Road was heavily traveled and represented an important overland artery. The last major engagement of the war was at Eutawville.

A small colony of French Huguenots settled in this area. Some of the homes were lost when Lake Marion was created. A number of beautiful homes in Eutawville and lovely old plantation homes out from Eutawville remain. The plantation homes are difficult to locate.

For more information to assist in locating the plantation homes, consult *South Carolina: A Guide to the Palmetto State* (An American Series). There are no pictures of the homes in that book, but it does provide assistance in locating them.

ST. JULIEN PLANTATION

Highway 6 between Santee and Eutawville

This Italian Renaissance home was built in 1850 on land that had been deeded to Joseph de St. Julien in 1736. History indicates that a St. Julien family arrived in Charles Town from France and moved up the Cooper River to the three 1,000-acre tracts given to Pierre St. Julien by the lord proprietor of England. Whether or not Joseph de St. Julien was a member of this family is not known.

The Gaillard family purchased the St. Julien property, and it was inherited by Thomas Porcher. He built the house and dependencies in the early 1850s for his son, Julius, and his wife, Mary Wickham Porcher. Julius was killed during the War Between the States. The home later belonged to the Frank Conner family and Fred Norris.

Italian Renaissance architecture was very unusual for this section of South Carolina. The windows of this white frame house are unique. There is a grouping of three windows facing south on the second floor of the *L*-shaped house and a similar grouping on the west side above the single-story wing. Downstairs on the south side are two windows. The wing has one window with sidelights and double shutters plus one single window. The shed roof of the one-story porch on the front of the house has a Chinese-style curve. The home is crowned with a sparkling red-tin roof which is accented by a red-brick chimney.

This working plantation is located about one-half mile from Eutawville. In the spring there is a sign just across the highway inviting customers to pick their own strawberries (for a price, of course). This is a private home.

Elloree

Elloree is a very small town but it has an historic house, which is unique in design, located on the main street. Population of Elloree is less than 1,000.

The area, a part of Orangeburg County, was probably first settled by Germans and French Huguenots. The town was first called Harlin City. Later, it was changed to Elloree, which means "home I love." Some have suggested that the name came from an old nineteenth-century song which contained the following words: "Oh Elloree, so dear to me, it is lost forever more! Our home was down in Tennessee before the cruel war! Then carry me back to Tennessee, back where I long to be! Among the fields of yellow corn to my darling Elloree."

THE SNIDER HOUSE

Highway 6

This house was moved from Charleston in 1876. It was built of heart pine using wooden peg construction. William J. Snider, the founder of the town of Elloree, built this house. It is the oldest residence remaining in the town.

Woodwork on the bay at the front of the house is placed diagonally forming an inverted *V* rather than being horizontal or vertical. Doric square columns front the two-story porches. Both upper and lower doors are double with side-lights and transoms.

Conway

Europeans visited in this area in 1526. The land was called Chicora by the Waccamaw Indians who lived here until the 1700s. Conway was first named Kingston in 1732 when Robert Johnson, the royal governor, developed a plan for the province. The first settlers arrived in 1735, and at that time this area was considered a part of Craven County. In 1767 the colony became a part of Georgetown District. New lines were drawn in 1785 establishing Kingston County. Later, the name was changed to Horry County in honor of Gen. Peter Horry, and the town of Kingston was subsequently renamed Conwayborough for Gen. Robert Conway.

C. P. QUATTLEBAUM HOUSE

219 Kingston Street

The exact date of the construction of this home is unknown, but a map made by Josiah Lewis and dated 1816 shows the house to be in existence. The land was acquired by Anthony Pawley in 1807. Thomas Durant purchased the property in 1822, and it was subsequently bought by Col. C. P. Quattlebaum in 1887. Cephas Perry Quattlebaum was born in the Lexington District, South Carolina, in 1851. He grew up during the difficult days of Reconstruction. He read law in the office of Maj. H. A. Meetze of Lexington and was admitted to the bar in 1874. Soon after that event he moved to Conwayborough. He worked diligently to rid the state of radical rule and was very active in the campaign to elect Governor Hampton. After the election the governor appointed him aide-de-camp to the commander in chief with the rank of lieutenant colonel. Later, Governor Simpson appointed him to a similar position.

Colonel Quattlebaum led the move to incorporate the town of Conway in 1898 and was the first mayor.

The home is of white frame construction and features a two-story, wraparound porch with decorative posts which are embellished with carved wooden brackets. The wing on the right has a bay window arrangement. There is an interesting cupola between the two gables. This is a private residence.

BEATY-SPIVEY HOUSE (THE OAKS)

428 Kingston Street

This was the home of Thomas Wilson Beaty, who signed the Ordinance of Secession and was, also, a senator from the Horry District. The Beaty family members were pioneer residents of Horry County. In 1851 Beaty married Mary Elizabeth Brookman, who was the governess of the children of Mr. Buck, a shipbuilder from Maine. Mary Elizabeth was born in Bucksport, Maine. She came to Bucksport, South Carolina in the 1840s to work for Mr. Buck. A shipbuilder working for Mr. Buck probably built this home.

Beaty fought in the War Between the States and left his wife in charge of his affairs. She supervised his businesses, which included mercantile and naval stores plus a newspaper. She became a very influential woman. They had five children and lost all five tragically: two drowned in the lake behind their house and two died with diphtheria when they were quite young. An oft-repeated story chronicles the death of Brookie, their only son. He is said to have been very ill and was in an upstairs room. Mary was in the parlor and heard beautiful music. Angels appeared to her which were in the likenesses of her daughters who had died previously. According to Mary, the girls said that they had come for their brother. Mary rushed upstairs to find the child dead.

A spacious lot provides a lovely setting for this home with huge oak trees surrounding it. The house is white frame construction and is most unusual. There is a very high gable in the center with two windows. Four Tuscan columns outline the one-tiered porch. All of the windows are single over single. The home has great balance with twin chimneys and one-story wings at each side. In later years the property was owned by the Col. D. A. Spivey family.

This is a private residence.

OLDE ENGLISH DISTRICT

Lancaster

There are seven counties in the Olde English District. This section will only present homes from Fairfield, Chester, York, Lancaster, and Union counties. The most interesting drive through this area is not by interstate highway but over the other less traveled roads.

The earliest settlers in this area were from Pennsylvania and were Scotch-Irish who were looking for a better life. The Church of England had made life unbearable for those of other faiths. Between 1760 and 1775 many immigrants arrived in South Carolina from Ireland. There was a "bounty system" to attract immigrants to the state.

WADE-BECKHAM HOUSE

The Wade-Beckham House is located approximately seven miles from Lancaster on S.C. 200 in Lancaster County. This is one of the seven counties in what is described as the Olde English District. As you travel through the countryside and small towns of the Olde English District, you will find Revolutionary and Civil War sites, historic buildings, and gardens. The Wade-Beckham House is one of the last remaining plantation homes. It is a two-story frame building that blends Greek Revival and neoclassical architecture. The columns on the front are an unusual feature. They are not attached to the gallery railings, the gallery, or any place on the house except at the top. At the bottom they go straight to the ground resting on a mortar base.

Built by James T. Wade sometime between 1802 and 1811, it was probably intended to be used as a summer home away from the low-lying areas. Later, the house belonged to James Rinaldo Massey, Jr., who was a state legislator from 1884 to 1885. The Beckham family inherited the home in 1905, and it has remained in the family since that time.

A visit impresses one with the effort to maintain the nineteenth-century decor. The rooms contain furniture dating back to the early 1800s which are family collections. The Wade Hampton Room is named for South Carolina's great statesman and contains historic military artifacts. The house was nearly doubled in size in 1915, but this room is a part of the original structure. Two other rooms, the Rose Room and the Summer House Room, contain interesting collections of antiques such as lacy fans, a pine armoire, and a hand-painted rose plate that was spared when Gen. William T. Sherman burned one of the family homes.

An interesting old store that was built about the turn of the century stands beside the home. It was moved to this location about 1930 and is now an antique store and gift shop.

Since the Wade-Beckham House is now a bed and breakfast inn, it is always open for visitors. Dr. and Mrs. William H. Duke are the current owners. Mrs. Duke is the daughter of H. J. Beckham, Jr.

Mrs. Duke writes, "I am sending a boiled custard recipe that was handwritten in an ancient cookbook that came into my possession. I used to love this stuff when I was a child."

Boiled Custard—A Family Recipe

Place a quart of milk in a pitcher and place in a kettle of cold water. When the water begins to boil, stir into the milk six eggs, well-beaten, with one and one-half teaspoons of salt and a tablespoon of sugar added. Stir constantly, and take it out of the kettle as soon as it is as thick as cream. Flavor with lemon.

Another dish served frequently by Mrs. Duke is Baked Cheese Grits.

1 cup grits (non-instant)	1 cup New York sharp
2 cups water	cheddar
1 cup milk	1/2 stick butter
1 teaspoon salt	Tabasco sauce (a few
Two eggs, beaten	drops)

Cook grits in water, milk, and salt. When thick, remove from heat and add cheese, butter, and Tabasco. Gradually add beaten eggs to the hot grits. Pour into a one and one-half quart greased casserole dish and bake in a 350-degree oven for thirty minutes or until the top is brown.

This may be prepared for baking twenty-four hours ahead. Then bring to room temperature before baking. Serves four to six.

Winnsboro

From Interstate 20 east of Columbia, take Highway 321 to Winnsboro. This town, in Fairfield County, was influenced by the English and the French Huguenots in Charleston. It became an early educational center in the state, and by 1796 there were twelve churches in the county. A ten-acre rock of solid granite was on Capt. James Kincaid's plantation. As a result of this discovery a quarry was operated by the Winnsboro Blue Granite Company.

Some of the points of interest are the Olde Town Clock (1833); the Fairfield County Court House, designed by Robert Mills and built in 1823; and many beautiful old churches. The Old Brick Church was erected in 1788 and is worthy of a visit. There are also approximately two hundred plantation homes in the county.

MCCREIGHT HOUSE
107 Vanderhurst Street

Built in 1774, approximately thirty-five years after the founding of Winnsboro, the McCreight House is probably the oldest house remaining in the town. There is evidence that it was the first house in this area not built of logs. As settlers moved from Charleston, a sophisticated city, they could not accept the log houses and demanded better homes. The fact that this frame house still stands may be due to the cabinetmaking skills of Col. William McCreight, the builder.

The construction style is referred to as a "raised cottage." Some think that this type of building was designed to raise the living quarters high above ground level because of mosquitos. Others suggest that it was to provide living space in the basement for the slaves while the family of white people lived on the second, and in this case, the third floor of the house.

There is a central stairway to the second level of the house with a porch across the front. On this second level there are four rooms with a central stairway leading to the third floor, where the bedrooms are located.

Mrs. Gene Smith Quattlebaum, the last owner of the house, deeded it to the town of Winnsboro on June 15, 1975.

KINCAID-ANDERSON HOME (HEYWARD HALL)

Landis Road

The Kincaid-Anderson Home reminds the visitor of an English country estate. This house is often referred to as "the castle." There is a serpentine wall surrounding the gardens and a magnificent avenue of trees that is 200 feet long. The builder used the pattern of the Castle Inverary, and the construction features solid brick walls with the Flemish bond.

Capt. James Kincaid, a Scottish nobleman, sailed from Ireland to Charleston in 1773. He went from there to Fairfield County and married within three months. He and his wife lived in a log cabin while their home was being built in 1774.

The bricks, nails, lumber, and all ornamentation came from England. The walls are as smooth as marble. The interior of the house was considered to be the finest in this section of South Carolina. The rooms are quite large with very high ceilings. The windows are nine over nine with dark shutters. The triangular pediment over the doorway makes the entry very elegant.

During the Revolutionary War the house became the meeting place for important people in the up-country. The place descended to the Anderson family through marriage.

Terraced gardens at the rear of the house lead down to Mill Creek in six levels. Each of these is supported by a massive block of stone.

Much of the beautiful interior of the house has been lost, but Daniel Heyward and the Blue Granite Company reconditioned it.

Kincaid-Anderson Home, now referred to as "Heyward Hall," is located about twelve miles southwest of Winnsboro, just off State Highway 213 on Landis Road. It is eight-tenths of a mile from the junction and on the left side of the road.

BRATTON PLACE (WYNNE DEE)

204 Bratton

Bratton Place has been the home of some of Winnsboro's most prominent families for more than two hundred years. It was built in 1781 on land that was part of an original land grant from King George of England to Joseph Owen in 1768. The land was surveyed by Richard Winn, a Royal Deputy Surveyor, who came from Virginia to settle in the area. Winnsboro was named for him. He persuaded Owen to sell the land to him, and in 1777 he deeded one hundred acres from his purchase for an academy.

Winn had an outstanding role in the revolution. He was associated with the battles of Fort Moultrie and Fort McIntosh, Georgia; and York and Hanging Rock near Lancaster. In 1780 he helped to defend Charleston.

He was twice elected lieutenant governor of South Carolina and served in the United States Congress from 1793 to 1797. Later he was re-elected and served from 1803 to 1813.

In 1805 the home and land were deeded to his daughter, Christine, as a wedding gift when she married Col. William Bratton. He was a member of a very important York County family. Gen. John Bratton, the son of Christine and William, served with Lee at Appomattox during the War Between the States. His wife, Betty DuBois of Roseland Plantation, took refuge at Bratton Place during those difficult months. On February 21, 1865, General Sherman moved his army to Winnsboro after burning Columbia. They drove their horses through the hallway of the house, breaking down the front door as well as the center stairway. The imprint of the horses' hooves can still be seen in the wide plank pine flooring.

There have been some changes made in the house, but the original part remains virtually unaltered. Both the interior and exterior walls are of heart pine and are held together with pegs and handwrought nails. The windows are nine over nine and still retain the original handblown glass.

The three chimneys are made from English ballast brick used to weight the ships sailing to this country from England. They were brought by oxcart from Charleston.

The design of the doorway is outstanding. The details (triangles and circles within the squares) in the sidelights involve all the various designs used in the colonial period. The pilasters are of the Adamesque style. The present door replaced the door torn out by Sherman's men in 1865.

The dadoes and trim inside the house were all done by hand. The Adam mantel "sunburst" design was carved with a penknife and gauge. It is paneled to the ceiling. In the dining room the hand-carved mantel is the Fan and Daisy design.

In the original part of the house are the "Christain" doors such as are found in the Scotch-Irish homes of the pioneer period. These doors have panels in a cross shape. The "lean-to hinges" are constructed in such a way as to allow the doors to swing open over the rugs.

From the patio the original outside kitchen may be seen. It was used until 1868, when a kitchen was added to the main part of the house.

Chester

Continue on Highway 321 to Chester. Chester County was settled by the Scotch-Irish Presbyterians from Pennsylvania in the 1750s, bringing with them such names as "Lancaster," "York," and "Chesterfield." Lewis Turnout, located seven miles from the town of Chester, was chosen in 1791 for the location of the county seat of government, and the Chester County courthouse was erected there. This was significant for the future of the town of Chester.

The homes of Chester County are not as grand as those of some other areas. Not many from Charleston spent their summers in Chester, so the homes remained the sturdy homes of working people. Chester is considered a typical "courthouse town." Cotton was an important crop, and the town is still an agricultural center. The War Between the States was not as devastating to Chester as to some other areas; the landowners knew how to work even though they owned slaves.

Chester is proud of its hometown image. In 1983 the movie *Chiefs* was filmed here. The moviemakers were attracted to the town by the general atmosphere, the historic buildings, and the old homes. There are a number of commercial buildings on Main Street which were erected in the 1800s. Beautiful, historic homes are found in the Historic District and along the highways leading out of Chester.

Anne P. Collins has written an interesting history of Chester County entitled *A Goodly Heritage*. In her book Collins, a veteran newspaper journalist, chronicles the history of the county in a style as easy to read as a novel.

THE WOOTEN HOUSE

Highway 72 East

The Wooten House is located in the area of the old Lewis Turnout community. The settlers of this area immigrated from Ireland and England. The more prominent names among them were Gill, Crawford, Lewis, Wherry, Caldwell, and Chisholm. The Wooten House was built by the Gill family on land that was a direct grant from King George III dated April 7, 1772, and at the same time a grant was given to the Wherry family. The actual date of the construction of the Wooten House is not known. The Wherry Plantation house was built in 1806, and it is thought that the Wooten House must have been built about the same time. The Rob Gill family had several sons who served in the Revolutionary War, and only two of them survived to return to Chester County.

One of the unusual features of the Wooten home was that the kitchen had no windows. There were just small openings large enough for the barrel of a gun which was used in defense against the Indians. The house is white frame with two front entrances. There is a small porch with six slender columns, and the porch railing is latticed. The house is flanked by matching brick chimneys of unusual design. The windows are six over six.

Dr. and Mrs. John C. Caldwell later owned the plantation. Other owners were Mr. and Mrs. Milton Wooten and Mr. and Mrs. Bill Wooten.

About two miles beyond the Lewis Turnout community on the right side of the road, watch for a sign on a black mailbox which reads, "Coach House, Farm and Stables." Turn at this sign. The house is at the top of the hill. It is not open to the public, but if the owner is out exercising horses she will very graciously tell you about her home.

THE WHERRY PLANTATION

Highway 72 East

Samuel Wherry was born in Ireland in 1734. He married Doris Coulter, also born in Ireland. When they came to America they settled first at Chester, Pennsylvania, and then in the 1760s they moved to South Carolina. The first records of land surveyed by Wherry were dated 1764. He received two land grants from King George III of England on April 7, 1772, with 100 acres in each grant. His son, Samuel Jr., built the plantation home in 1806. He was born in 1775 in Chester County and worked as a blacksmith. To the union of Samuel Wherry, Jr., and Sarah Ferguson one child, James Ferguson Wherry, was born. Six generations of Wherrys have lived in this beautiful home.

Claudia Wherry Mayben, daughter of James Ferguson Wherry II, refers to the house as "the old colonial home." The house of white frame seems to have been originally a large two-story rectangular building with a double portico in the middle at the front. There are four square pillars on both levels with Doric capitals and both upper and lower railings are a woven diamond-pattern latticework. The roof has a wide overhang across the front with brackets attached to the molding which appears to be lowered about fifteen inches from the top. The molding and paneling on the portico are very lovely, and a window is located in the eaves of the roof. The front door is massive with sidelights and a transom light. The windows are also quite large with six-over-six panes and flanking shutters. The home was remodeled in 1824 by James Ferguson Wherry I.

Until recently, the property was jointly owned by members of the Wherry family. Apparently, at this point it has been rented. This is one of the most beautiful places in the Chester area. Hopefully, it will be preserved. It is exactly one-half mile from the Wooten House and one and one-half miles from Highway 909. It is not open to the public.

LEWIS INN

Highway 909

The town of Lewis Turnout was incorporated shortly after the War Between the States and was the county seat of Chester County for a brief period of time. There were two barrooms and a jail. A man by the name of McHaffey was mayor during Reconstruction, and Lewis Gill, a black man, was the policeman. There were two aldermen who were both black. During a campaign for governor, one of the aldermen was shot for cheering for her candidate. The white people of Lewis Turnout petitioned Judge Walker to withdraw the charter and that ended the town of Lewis Turnout, but it has remained a village.

Just off Highway 72 East on Highway 909 in the town of Lewis Turnout was Lewis Inn. It provided overnight accommodations for travelers. When Aaron Burr was being taken to trial, he managed to escape as they passed through the town of Chester. He pleaded for help from the people of Chester, declaring his innocence, but the guards apprehended him and took him out to Lewis Inn. There was a bench on the front porch, and they secured him to this bench where he was forced to sleep that night. This bench is now in the Chester Museum.

The Inn is now a charming country cottage. The present owners have restored the building, and colorful plants, shrubs, and a huge old oak tree frame the house. Shutters cover the front windows. The windows on the gable ends of the house are two over two on the upper level and six over six on the lower. A porch across the front is supported by six columns. The front features stick bannisters and brick steps. This is a private residence.

J. S. JACKSON HOUSE
124 York Street

The modest white frame house at 124 York in Chester is one of the town's most unusual. It has a Greek Revival porch with square posts built at the edge of the sidewalk. The steps are at one end. Latticed balustrades were not often used during this period in South Carolina, but there are three homes in Chester, including the Jackson House, using this feature. Brick chimneys flank each end of the home. The windows are six over six with plantation-style shutters. Several years ago when the house was refloored, it was discovered that the foundation was of tree trunks that still had the bark on them.

The kitchen was built with wooden pins and located in the backyard. The wooden pins were revealed when the kitchen was moved to join the main house. Mr. R. C. West bought the lot in 1855, and William T. Robinson then built the home on this lot. Later owners were Mr. and Mrs. J. S. Jackson, by whose name the house is known.

This is a private residence.

JUDGE GAGE HOUSE

143 York Street

York is a street of tall trees and beautiful old homes. The Judge Gage House is one of the most attractive. Originally, the bricks were red, but they are now painted white. Absolom Housar built this modified Georgian-style residence sometime before 1855. There were two rooms on each side of a hall on both levels. Housar suffered a reversal in his financial affairs and lost his home. It was sold in a sheriff's sale in 1858 to James Hemphill for $2,050. Hemphill, an attorney, lived here with his family for a very short period. During that time he drastically changed the looks of the house by adding blinds to the windows and a two-story piazza. The large square columns and pediment are very impressive. Mr. J. Lucius Gaston purchased the property in 1859 for $3,000. Captain Gaston was killed in the War Between the States, and his widow and children continued to live in the home.

Judge Gage married Mrs. Gaston's daughter and enlarged the house. Originally, the kitchen was in the backyard, but a kitchen was included as part of the wing which Mr. Gage added. The home remained in the Gaston family for many years. Gaston Gage, the grandson of Mrs. Gaston, sold the home to Mr. and Mrs. Cody Quinton.

The home is private.

BRAWLEY HOUSE

145 York Street

Major Kennedy built this house on York Street in 1838 for Mr. and Mrs. Hiram Brawley. It remained in the Brawley family until 1923, when it was purchased by Mrs. Davidson. Lettie Crawford was a later owner.

There are two levels to the house, and it is built on a full basement. The wide verandah across the front features slender round columns supporting the roof. Guests are welcomed by a beautiful front door that has sidelights. Above it there is a fanlight with a sunburst design. When houses of this style were built, the basement was used for dining and the bedrooms, living room, and reception area were on the other two floors. This is a private residence.

Brattonsville

Take Highway 322 east to Brattonsville in York County. York County was settled by Scotch-Irish also. They had a democratic spirit that would inevitably lead them into involvement in the Revolutionary and Civil wars. After the fall of Charleston, all of South Carolina fell to the British except York County. The people organized and successfully turned back the British at the Battle of Brattonsville. Soon thereafter the Battle of King's Mountain followed, and the British were decisively defeated. Many believe this to have been the turning point of the war.

The King's Mountain State Park and the King's Mountain National Military Park are located on State Highway 161 just sixteen miles northwest of York. A visit to the National Park is a must. The Museum of York County in Rock Hill is unusual, containing hundreds of artifacts from centuries past. It houses the world's largest collection of mounted, hooved African mammals.

The York Historic District contains many interesting old homes with a wide variety of building styles. The streets are tree-lined and well maintained. York was the first town in the up-country to have gaslights.

Brattonsville is a village that has been preserved. Self-guided tours of the town are offered.

BRATTONSVILLE

Brattonsville Road

Here in 1760 settled the brothers, William, Robert and Hugh Bratton, who fought in the Revolutionary War. One quarter mile east of James Williamson's was fought the battle of Williamson Plantation on July 12, 1780. The outnumbered patriot militia, led by Colonel William Bratton and Captain John McClure, surprised and defeated a superior force of British troops commanded by Captain Christain Houk, who was killed during the fighting. In the subsequent route and pursuit, Colonel Bratton's house became the scene of action. This was the first check to the British since the fall of Charleston. . . .

These statements are taken from the marker in front of the Bratton Plantation Home in historic Brattonsville, but there is much more to the story. Here one sees how a family of very meager means through hard work and ambition progressed from a very small, primitive cottage to a beautifully appointed "plantation home."

The Bratton family, over several generations, have restored a village of eighteenth- and nineteenth-century structures. A foundation, Friends of Historic Brattonsville, has continued the work. Historic Brattonsville is an ongoing research and restoration center which is open to the public. The visitor's center is located in an old home that was moved from Chester to the site and then restored and remodeled for this use.

A self-guided tour leads from the most primitive back-woodsman's cabin to the McConnell House, which is a restored cabin not quite as primitive. There are a number of buildings on the site which have been moved from other locations, and together they provide a good picture of life in the eighteenth and early nineteenth centuries. The oldest house in York County is the Colonel Bratton house, which was built in 1776. The land was a grant from King George III. The Brattons lived in this house for many years. The furnishings indicate that by the time this home was occupied the family was becoming more affluent. A beautiful sideboard built in 1847 by someone in the area graces the dining room.

Dr. John Simpson Bratton lived here after the death of his parents. About 1823, he built the home across the road. There were four rooms originally. The ceilings on the first level are twelve feet high and upstairs they are ten feet high. The windows are nine over nine. Shortly after its construction, two wings were added, and the parlor was extended. Everything used in the building was made on the premises. Bratton was one of the largest slave owners in the area. Very few people were able to live in the style of the Brattons—they were highly cultured, and music was extremely important in their lives. On entering the central hall one is confronted with a stairway ascending to the second and third levels. The library and a bedroom are on the right. On the left are a parlor with two fireplaces with lovely mantels and a breakfast room. Some of the furniture in the home belonged to the Bratton family, and all of it is from the period during which the house was built. There are four large bedrooms upstairs. The wainscoting in the upper hall and in one of the bedrooms is red and gold.

Dr. and Mrs. Bratton had fourteen children with that number being divided equally between boys and girls. Wishing to have their children educated, Bratton began a school in the small house. He added a large schoolroom at the side of the house and employed Schoolmaster Ladd, who lived with the family in the home. Friends of the Brattons sent their children to the "Ladd Female Academy," and some of the students boarded with the Brattons. Sometimes there were as many as twenty-eight people living in the house.

Behind the residence and made of red brick is the only detached dining room in the United States. It is connected to the main structure with a breezeway. The room was used every day for all meals. It is a beautiful room with a fanlight over the entry door. The basement was used as a general workroom. The "dumbwaiter" that was used to send food up to the dining room has been removed.

Other buildings in the Brattonsville village are the doctor's office, a store built in 1870, and a lovely red-brick house built in 1843 which eventually housed the school. These two buildings are still owned by the Brattons. They are being restored at this time and will, in all probability, be open to the public at some point in the future.

Brattonsville is open to the public several days each week. Call 803-684-2327 for information. Take Highway 321 to Highway 322. Four miles beyond that point, Brattonsville Road appears on the right. Two miles up this road the traveler will find Brattonsville and will conclude that it was certainly worth the trip. There is an admission charge.

HIGHTOWER HALL

Brattonsville Road

When traveling the highways of South Carolina, there are many surprises. Hightower Hall is one of those delightful surprises. Located on the Brattonsville Road near McConnells in York County is this beautiful Italian-villa-style home. Hightower Hall is a two-story white frame house with a three-story tower in the center extending ten feet above the roof. It was built in 1863 by John Simpson Bratton II. The contractor was O. P. Cranford (or Crawford). The Homestead, the Brick House, and Hightower Hall are three lovely homes built by Bratton in this immediate vicinity.

Bratton was a prominent planter and politician and was apparently a wealthy man by the time he built Hightower Hall. He probably owned between seventy-five and one hundred slaves and a significant amount of property. He served in the South Carolina House of Representatives for two terms, was postmaster of Brattonsville, and was a member of the Soldiers Board of Relief during the War Between the States. Bratton died in 1888. The first Brattons were Revolutionary War heroes, and the later Brattons were Confederate heroes.

The Italian villa style was popular in the United States from 1837 to 1860. It originated with the farmhouses of northern Italy. The first house of this style to be built in the United States was in 1837 at Burlington, New Jersey. It was designed by architect John Notman.

The high square tower identifies Hightower Hall as an example of the Italian villa style of architecture. There are twin porches, one on each side of the tower, resting on high brick piers and featuring square posts. The decorative, scroll-saw trim was a forerunner of the "dripping lace" of the later Victorian period. On each floor the tower has a single eight-over-eight window with shutters. Windows in other parts of the house are also eight over eight with shutters. One of the significant features of the first floor central hall is the trompe l'oeil painting which resembles marble columns or pilasters. It is unknown how this art came to York County. There is a possibility that an English designer may have decorated the house. A similar painting style is found in Alison Plantation in York County. Lovely chandeliers, medallions, and plasterwork add to the beauty of the home.

In addition to the house, there are two barns and two slave cabins.

To locate the house, travel along Highway 321 to Highway 322. Follow 322 to Brattonsville Road. Hightower Hall is a short distance down this road, and being such an outstanding structure it is easily identified.

This house is private.

Union

After Brattonsville travel the opposite direction on Highway 322 to State Highway 49. Continue to Union, crossing the Broad River. Rivers almost completely surround this county. The first settlers were from Virginia and Pennsylvania arriving in 1745, and they built their homes along the banks of these rivers. Indians were still a threat at that time.

The settlers built the Union Church on the banks of Brown's Creek, and all denominational groups worshipped here. When the county was formed in 1785 the name Union was chosen. Soon cotton became the major crop, and the county became one of the most prosperous in the United States. In 1811 a free school was organized for children whose parents could not afford private schools.

Three governors of the state came from Union County. They were William Gist, David Johnson, and Thomas B. Jeter. When Sherman occupied Columbia, the state offices were moved to Union. Governor McGrath worked in the library of "The Shrubs," the home of Colonel Dawkins.

Elaborate homes with Greek Revival facades and huge columns across the front were built with the wealth generated from the cotton plantations. Some refer to Union County as "The County of Colonnades." The circular stairways, spacious rooms with high ceilings, and sparkling chandeliers became symbols of an affluent way of life for this new aristocracy.

The War Between the States destroyed much of the wealth of this prosperous area but in 1893 the first cotton mill in the county helped to restore some of its former glory. The Union Buffalo Mill became the largest such mill in the United States. Mill workers replaced slave labor.

Some of the most beautiful houses in the state are found in Union County. On South Street in the little picturesque city of Union there are antebellum and Victorian homes. Rose Hill mansion is located on State Road 16, eight miles south of Union, and is open to the public. On Neal Shoals Road the Meador Plantation can be found, along with other stately mansions.

ROSE HILL

Old Buncomb Road

Rose Hill is probably the most notable plantation home in Union County. It was built in 1826 by William Henry Gist, governor of South Carolina. This Greek-style, three-story, brick home has walls twenty-eight inches thick. Sometime after 1860, the bricks were covered with stucco, and two-story piazzas were added in both the front and the back. Four square Doric posts support a triangular pediment on the front. Entrance doors on both levels have sidelights and fanlights. Windows are flanked by dark-green shutters.

Furniture once belonging to the Gist family is found in what is now known as Rose Hill State Park. Governor Gist's former bedroom contains his own tester bed, wardrobe, and leather trunk. Mrs. Gist's wedding gown and bonnet are in a display cabinet in the ballroom. Other pieces such as bric-a-brac, a bust of Governor Gist, and a portrait of General "States Rights" Gist are appropriately used in decorating the home.

Governor Gist was born in Charleston in 1809 and moved to Union County in 1819. He became a wealthy planter and lawyer. He built Rose Hill when he married Louisa Bowen of Laurens, and he lived in this home until his death—the last governor to live in his own home while in office. Prior to his term as governor, he served as a state representative, state senator, and lieutenant governor. Toward the end of his term of office in 1860, the Secession Movement was becoming stronger each day. The governor sent his cousin, "States Rights" Gist, to visit other Southern governors to determine their sentiments related to this issue. They were in sympathy with the stand taken in South Carolina. Therefore, Governor Gist called upon the General Assembly to request a convention of the people to meet in Columbia on December 17, 1860, which was the day his term expired. Governor Gist was elected a delegate from Union and was one of the signers of the Ordinance of Secession when it was executed in Charleston on December 20.

The house is open to the public and is located nine miles south of the Union County Courthouse off of Highway 49.

CROSS KEYS

Old Buncomb Road at James Ford Road

Built over the period from 1812 to 1814 by Barnum Bobo, this house is a good example of Georgian Colonial. Just a short distance from Cross Keys on Highway 49 is a marker for this house and for Rose Hill. The structure is easily seen from Highway 49. The bricks used on this tall, two-story home appear to have been handmade. In addition to the two main levels, there are an attic and a basement. Identical chimneys stand at each of the gabled ends. There are five windows of nine over nine across the upper floor and two on each side of the front entry. Huge white Tuscan columns support the triangular pediment of the raised front portico. A date stone placed beneath one of the gables has the date "1814," the owner's initials, "B. B.," and crossed keys which were thought to be the insignia of the builder.

Diaries contain evidence that Jefferson Davis, his cabinet, and his military escort dined here on their flight from Richmond. Those with Davis were: General Ferguson of Mississippi; Generals Dibrell and Vaughn of Tennessee; Col. W. C. P. Breckenridge and Gen. Basil Duke of Kentucky; Gen. John Breckenridge; and General Bragg, Senior General of the Army.

There is a historic marker in front of the house.

MEADOR PLANTATION
Neal Shoals Road

Massive columns that rest on square posts front this lovely red-brick plantation home. The triangular pediment above the two-tiered portico features a Palladian window and dentil molding. The cornice also has dentil molding. Twin red-brick chimneys frame the roof of the original part of the house. Windows upstairs are six over six and downstairs are six over nine; the shutters on all the windows are white. In the early years of this home the kitchen and slave quarters were housed in the basement. There are two floors above the basement as well as a large room on the attic level.

The interior features a wide central hall on both levels with rooms on each side. Each hall opens into rooms across the rear, forming a *T*. The floor of the basement is laid with ten-inch square bricks that were made on the premises, but the bricks of the walls were imported from England. Wings were added to each end of the house in this century. The home was built in 1852 for Austin Wilson. Then, in 1856, Dr. William P. Thompson purchased the property and in just one year sold it to John Meador.

When the defeated Confederate soldiers were wearily traveling home on foot through South Carolina and saw this home dramatically located atop a hill, their spirits rose. They hoped to be able to sleep in the barn or be given a meal. When they knocked on the door to ask permission to sleep in the barn John Meador insisted that those tired men sleep in the house and enjoy a fine breakfast. Many Confederate soldiers had fond memories of this place.

A. D. Meador bought the home and 700 acres of land in 1926. It has remained in the Meador family from 1857 until just recently. This is a private home.

GOVERNOR JETER HOUSE

203 Thompson Boulevard

This home, built for Gov. Thomas Jeter, is a perfect example of pre-Victorian architecture. Other than modern conveniences, it remains unaltered. Scroll-saw scalloped trim outlines the shape of this frame house with its porches in the front, sides, and back. The gabled side features a double bay. The upper bay has graceful ogee arches, and the lower bay has windows that are six over nine. The windows elsewhere are double and narrow with four over four, and all are flanked by dark shutters.

The two-story house is on a raised foundation, but there is a basement under only one room. The builder used the central hall plan which was used in so many houses built in South Carolina during this era. The spiral staircase at the rear of the hall is probably one of the finest in Union County. It follows the curve of the apsidal (semicircular) wall. The door under the stairway leading to the back porch is slanted to fit under the stairs. The hall plan with the apsidal wall is similar to that of Merridun; it is thought that the same carpenters or maybe even the same architect built this home after building Merridun.

To the right of the hall is the very spacious dining room with walnut cornices over the windows. The same types of cornices are in the three upstairs bedrooms. The parlor is across the hall. The twelve-foot ceiling in this room is decorated with finely detailed molded plasterwork in the strawberry and leaf design and the egg and dart pattern. The cornices above the windows are gold-leafed pressed tin. This decorative work combines to create a beautiful room.

Just behind this is a small room that the present owner believes may have been Governor Jeter's office. It has a door that opens onto one of the side porches. The cornices are identical to those in the parlor. The home was built with closets in every room, which was almost unheard of when this was built in 1859. There are three bells at the rear of the house with a system of bellpulls in each room which were used to summon the servants. The original kitchen is now a guesthouse.

The Jeter family owned the home until 1905, when it was purchased by the Sarratt family. Mrs. Whitener, a descendant of the Sarratts, later bought the house.

MERRIDUN

22 Merridun Street

William Keenan built this beautiful and elegant mansion in 1855, and Benjamin H. Rice purchased the property in 1876. It has been occupied by Rice descendants until recently when it was bought to be converted into a bed and breakfast inn.

Thomas Carey Duncan, a grandson of Rice, was a well-known Union County political and industrial leader. He built the first industrial mill when he established Union Cotton Mill in 1893. Three years later, he established the Union Buffalo Mill. Duncan also constructed the Union and Glenn Springs Railroad and the hydroelectric plant at Neal Shoals. He served in the South Carolina House of Representatives, the South Carolina Senate, and as mayor of Union.

When first built, Merridun was a simple Georgian-style house. The two-storied columned portico and the first-floor verandah which wraps around the side were added about the turn of the century. Duncan replaced the Doric columns with Corinthian columns in 1911. The home now presents a Classic Revival appearance.

The interior has a central hall with rooms on each side, which is known as the Georgian Plan. At the rear of the hallway is a curved staircase that fits into the apsidal wall. A semicircular arched door leads to the rear verandah. The windows of the first floor are six over nine, extend almost to the floor, and are flanked by dark shutters. The front entry has fluted pilasters and an ornate pediment. Ceilings are very high, and the floors are heart pine. In a city that is noted for its colonnaded houses, this one stands out as probably the most beautiful.

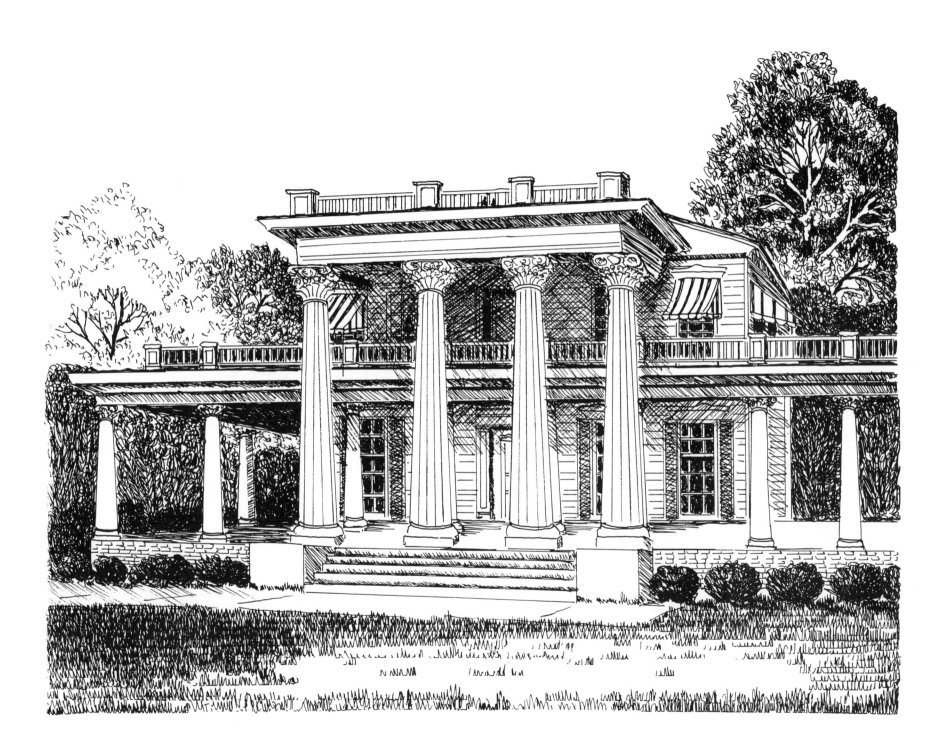

THE PIEDMONT

Spartanburg

The first people to visit Spartanburg were likely Spanish explorers in 1567. Many years ago a stone was found by a farmer near Spartanburg with the date 1567 scratched into it as well as a rectangle with a rising sun. It is thought to have been left by Juan Pardo and is probably the oldest European artifact in South Carolina.

Spartanburg County is known as the "Peach Capital of the World." Within the last half of a century the city has become the location of major industrial installations. The city is an educational center with three four-year colleges and one junior college. The beautiful churches in the area reflect the fact that religion plays an important part in the lives of the citizens.

The Spartan Regiment fought bravely in the Revolutionary War. The name "Spartanburg" is thought to have been chosen in an effort to honor this military unit. The county was originally a part of the old Ninety-Six District and became a county in 1785.

WALNUT GROVE PLANTATION

1200 Otis Shoal Road

Charles Moore was granted land by King George III amounting to about three thousand acres. Originally from Ireland, Moore settled in the Spartanburg area after a stay in Pennsylvania in the 1760s. The land has been in the Moore family since that time; it is located on the Tyger River. The house, built in 1765 of unchinked logs, was later covered with clapboard. It has paneling that was the finest in the county for that period. The house has double shouldered chimneys with Queen Anne mantels. The two-story house has a porch across the front featuring square posts. The balusters are of stick-style construction. In the upper level windows are six over six, and those on the lower level are nine over nine.

Several other buildings are preserved on the farm. There is a separate kitchen, a blacksmith's forge, a meat house, and the Rocky Springs Academy. Dr. Andrew Barry Moore was the county's first doctor, and his office is located on the property.

Kate, the wife of Capt. Andrew Barry Moore, planted the walnut trees in approximately 1800. As a consequence the plantation soon became known as Walnut Grove. Kate Barry was a Revolutionary War heroine. When Daniel Morgan realized that he would have to confront Tarleton, he sent out couriers to round up his men. Kate tied Little Kate to the bedpost and left her alone while she rode her horse through part of her husband's beat, calling the men to take up arms.

Kate is buried in the family cemetery about five hundred yards west of the house.

The Spartanburg County Historical Association, with the help of the Junior League, restored the house and attendant buildings. The home is now open to the public Tuesday through Saturday all day and on Sunday from 2:00 to 5:00 P.M., April 1 through October 31. There is an admission charge.

There is a sign giving directions which is located on Highway 221 east of the Moore exit off of Interstate 26. Otis Shoal Road is one mile off Highway 221. The route is well marked.

Walnut Grove Plantation is listed in the National Historic Register.

JAMES BEVINGS HOME
North Church Street

In the 1830s Dr. James Bevings built a large cotton factory where he pioneered cotton manufacturing on a large scale. This area came to be known as Bevingsville. Cotton manufacturing continued there until the mid-twentieth century. Bevings pioneered the concept of the mill village and held very high standards for his workers. He later took over a mill in Crawfordville. He sold it in 1856, and that same year moved into this beautiful home in Spartanburg. The home later passed to the Evins family. John H. Evins was a congressional representative from Spartanburg in the 1870s and 1880s and was a highly influential politician in the state.

The tremendous white columns across the front are Greek Doric. The balustrade on the upper and lower gallery has diamond and bow-knot design, and there are brackets under the eaves across the front. The house is on a raised foundation sitting on a hillside well back from the street and under a grove of trees.

The house, a private dwelling, was listed in the National Historic Register in 1970.

BONHAVEN (CLEVELAND HOUSE)

North Church Street and Old Asheville Highway

Two of the most elegant mansions built here in the 1880s were built for the Cleveland brothers, John B. and Dr. Jesse. The latter built his house on Howard Street and John built his on North Church Street at the intersection of Old Asheville Highway. The houses were identical. The one on Howard Street was later destroyed.

The Cleveland brothers were involved in business ventures in and around Spartanburg. In fact, their names appear on the board of directors lists of almost all the companies in the area. John identified himself in the city directory as "capitalist." Jesse eventually quit his medical practice to manage his business affairs. The brothers were very close; an indication of that special relationship is reflected in the fact that each named his first son for his brother.

Bonhaven was built in 1889, and its central tower creates a structure much like the Italian-villa-style homes, except for its mansard roof. It would probably be classified as Second Empire style, an ornate eclectic style in America from the 1860s through the 1880s, named after the French Second Empire of Napoleon III.

The pillars were imported from Greece. The "Tea House," a small brick building used as a welcoming house, was imported from England. There are twenty-two rooms in this castle-like mansion.

Because of the density of the trees surrounding the house, it is almost impossible to view it except in the winter months. The Clevelands are very prominent in Spartanburg, and the home has remained in the family. It is in the National Historic Register, but is not open to the public.

FOSTER'S TAVERN

Highway 56 at Highway 295

This beautiful, historic home was three years in building, 1807 to 1810. The bricks were made at a location within sight of the home. Anthony Foster, Jr., was the builder and was an outstanding early settler. The walls of the house are from eighteen to twenty-four inches thick. The mansion was constructed with great taste as revealed by several features such as the "twin tied" brick chimneys of American Gothic or Tudor style. The portico entrance features a fan-shaped pedimented doorway and a second-floor balcony, and the roof line of this portico is pierced by the columns that extend from the gabled front to the ground. Inside, the mantels are rare bow fronts.

During the stagecoach days this tavern was a popular stop, and one of the frequent visitors was John C. Calhoun. He and many other notable people slept under this roof. The four large columns and the portico were added in 1845, and the side piazzas were built about 1915.

This is a private home.

THE PRICE HOUSE

Highway 199

Thomas Price went to Spartanburg District from York District about 1790. About four years later he bought 2,000 acres of land near Switzer and built his home near the fork of the South Tyger River and Ferguson Creek. The red-brick house is two and one-half stories with a high-pitched gambrel roof, a roof type that was characteristic of Delaware, Maryland, and eastern Pennsylvania. The bricks are laid in the Flemish bond. The interior walls are finished with an inch-thick coat of clay and lime that has been mixed with hair and flax. The inside chimney at each end of the building is unique for this area.

There is an exhibit of Price's original journals in the house. He not only farmed with his twenty-eight slaves, but he operated a store, post office, and had a license for "a house of entertainment." This gave him the right to house and feed travelers and their horses. The establishment was called a "public house."

The Price house has been restored by the Spartanburg County Historical Association, using the journals as guides to furnishing the house with items unique to the period. The Association now operates it as a house museum.

The best way to find the home is to take the Moore exit from Interstate 26 and proceed west on this highway to Switzer Church of God. Turn left at the church and find the house five and two-tenths miles down the road at the junction of State Roads 42-199, 42-86, and 42-200. It is easy to locate.

For additional information, contact the Spartanburg County Historical Association. The house is listed in the National Historic Register.

THE JAMMIE SEAY HOUSE

106 Darby Road

There is conflicting information as to the date this log cabin was constructed. The earliest date is 1760 and the latest is 1790, but whichever is correct, this is probably the oldest house in Spartanburg. The acre of land is thought to be a part of an original grant. Standing on the crest of a hill, the house probably has the best view in the city. The oldest part of the house is built of hand-hewn logs and then it was covered with wooden sheathing. The foundation and the chimney are of fieldstone, and the chimney has some brick at the top. This type of chimney is unusual in South Carolina, but is common in Virginia.

Jammie Seay, a Revolutionary War soldier, was born in Virginia in 1750. He fought in battles in Virginia, Pennsylvania, and South Carolina. The first grant in his name is dated 1784 for property near Fairforest Creek.

The house continued to be in possession of his descendants until the Spartanburg County Historical Association purchased it in 1974. Many people contributed toward the restoration of the house, including the National Preservation Society. In 1979, the Historical Association was presented an award for this house by the Auxiliary of the American Association of Architects for the most outstanding restoration in the state. The furnishings in the house are original or are of the period.

The house is open by appointment, and there is an admission charge. Call the Historical Association.

From downtown Spartanburg, go west on Church Street (Highway 221) to Crescent Avenue and turn right. Darby Road intersects Crescent. Watch for the street sign on the right.

This house is listed in the National Historic Register.

GEORGIA CLEVELAND HOUSE

162 North Dean Street

In 1904, the City Council voted a fifty-dollar-a-month appropriation to begin the first hospital in Spartanburg. The Spartanburg Hospital, erected on North Dean Street in 1905, was founded by Dr. Hugh Black. This was the first public hospital and employed the first laboratory technician in Spartanburg. After the Spartanburg General Hospital was built in 1921, the Spartanburg Hospital closed. The building later became the Georgia Cleveland House, a residential facility for older women of limited income which was founded in 1895. Residents said the atmosphere was truly that of a real home.

The three-story building is of red brick with "rosy" beige quions at the corners. The entrance features a small portico with Doric columns. Because of a single dormer on the roof, the home resembles the Italian villa style. The woodwork under the eaves is particularly lovely. There are double parlors and porches on two floors. The house is located directly behind First Baptist Church and is open to the public.

Greenville

Some say that Greenville was named to honor Revolutionary War hero Gen. Nathanael Greene, but others insist that the city was named for Isaac Green, an early settler. It is one of the largest cities in the state.

At one time Greenville was known as the "Textile Capital of the World." Although textiles are still a vital part of the economy of this area the industries are now highly diversified. The entire world's supply of Pepto-Bismol is produced at Procter and Gamble's plant in Greenville. Wilson sports equipment and tennis balls are produced exclusively here.

Greenville has several highly respected schools including Bob Jones University and Furman University, one of the finest privately endowed schools east of the Mississippi. The museum of sacred art on the campus of Bob Jones University houses one of the most outstanding collections of religious art in the world. Greenville County Museum of Art boasts an impressive collection, and the Peace Center for the Performing Arts provides many cultural enrichment opportunities.

WHITE HALL

310 West Earle Street

White Hall stands on what was once a 1,000-acre tract purchased by Elias Earle in 1796. Gov. Henry Middleton bought the tract in 1813. Prior to being elected governor, he was a member of the South Carolina House of Representatives and the United States Senate. He owned Middleton Place Gardens in Charleston, and his father was a signer of the Declaration of Independence.

Probably built in 1820 as a summer home, White Hall has the appearance of a typical country home of that era. The house is much like the Barbadian-style homes in Beaufort and Charleston with its wide verandah that wraps around the side of the house. Columns line the full length of these piazzas with smaller ones on the second level. On the ends of the house there are gables and wide stuccoed chimneys. The gardens around the house form a lovely frame.

The house is opened occasionally for garden tours.

ELIAS EARLE HOME

107 James Street

The Elias Earle home and Whitehall are the only surviving homes of the early 1800s within the city limits of Greenville. The date of the construction of this house was probably 1810. Records indicate that Earle took up lands in this section in 1787 and purchased the home site in 1796. The deed states that he lived on the site, so it is possible that the construction on the house was begun in 1796.

Moving to Greenville soon after the Revolutionary War, the Earle family was one of the earliest pioneer families in this area. Earle's father was one of the first members of the Virginia House of Burgesses. Later, Elias was a state senator from the Greenville District, a United States congressman, a silk grower, a manufacturer, and an ironmonger. He manufactured guns for the War of 1812. He was also the builder of the wagon trail across the Blue Ridge Mountains. Earle was born in Virginia in 1762. He is buried in the old Earle Cemetery on the plantation about one and one-half miles from the two houses.

"The Earle Town House" is built in the Palladian or early Georgian style. It is a frame dwelling painted white. Double steps lead the way to the handsome front door, which is surrounded by ornate woodwork, sidelights, and a transom. Above the door on the second level is a Palladian window. There are two nine-over-nine windows on each side of it; all windows are flanked by dark shutters. The tin-covered roof is a hip style, and there are twin chimneys. The woodwork within the house on the mantels, the paneled dado, the window, and door trim is carved.

The house is a private dwelling, but is open to the public occasionally for tours.

Laurens

Driving on Main Street of the charming little city of Laurens could be compared favorably with taking a journey into the past. Very large colonial, white, frame houses are intermingled with ornate Victorian homes sporting white "dripping lace" gingerbread trim. There are also some simplified Georgian-style homes. Dates of construction of these range from the early nineteenth century to the early twentieth century. Just a few blocks from Main Street, on Harper Street, is one of the oldest houses in Laurens, and other lovely, old homes can be seen on this street. In the oldest part of the city there are surprises around each corner with old homes tucked in here and there. Greystone Inn, a very good gourmet restaurant, is located in one of the old homes.

Laurens County was made a separate district in 1785. Prior to this it had been a part of the huge Craven County, which covered most of the state. Henry Laurens was a very important person in the government during the Revolution. His name was chosen for this district.

THE VILLA

Ball Drive

On January 11, 1837, Col. John Drayton Williams bought approximately 230 acres of land, located a short distance from West Main Street, for $3,500. Construction of this home did not begin until 1859, and it was completed in 1861. Williams owned two other homes. His second wife, Anna Eliza Barnett, inherited the property at his death. In 1874 Mrs. Williams remarried and in 1875 sold this home to Col. B. W. Ball, an attorney.

The next owner of the house was Mason Copeland, Ball's son-in-law. Sarah Ball Copeland and her daughter continued to live there for a long time; then the Copelands sold The Villa and surrounding land to Clyde Franks. The home had deteriorated through the years, and Franks was very interested in restoring this lovely old house. This was not the only home he restored, for he was always interested in building houses. He also had an interest in furniture. He was probably the leading person involved in preservation in Laurens County. The work on The Villa was completed in 1960 and in 1965 it became the residence of Franks, his wife, the former Sadie Fuller, and their family.

When Franks' sister, Martha, was retiring as a missionary to China, he built her a lovely little brick home near The Villa and gave her five acres of land. After Mr. Franks' death, Mrs. Franks continued to live in the small brick house until 1973, when she sold it to the Carl B. Smith family. The South Carolina Baptist Ministries for the Aging Inc. purchased the property in 1979 for the site of a retirement center. It was named the Martha Franks Retirement Center in honor of the veteran missionary.

The architect of The Villa is unknown. It was the only Italian-style villa in the Laurens area at that time. The structure is three stories high and the walls are of handmade brick overlaid with stucco. The outside walls are thirty-six inches thick; the inside walls, also of handmade brick covered with plaster, are fourteen inches thick. There are twelve rooms, the ceilings of which are sixteen feet high. Heart pine is used throughout the house. The beautiful and elaborate moldings were probably carved by slaves, as Mr. Williams was a wealthy planter and owned many slaves at the time of construction. The windows are tall and pedimented. There are four wings to the home with an outside entry to each. The profile of the house is dominated by two towers: one is located in the center and is ideal for lighting, and the other may have been a lookout tower from which to view the countryside in search of approaching Indians. The home is shaded and cooled by a wide piazza around it.

The Villa is currently used as the administrative office building and reception center of the retirement facility. The home has been restored beautifully, and its original structure has been maintained with integrity. Visitors should make advance appointments.

THOMAS BADGETT HOUSE
Highway 49

The Greek Revival house of Thomas Badgett, built in 1845, is in a square, Georgian design. The portico with columns gives the house the appearance of a Greek temple. It is thought that the entrance was taken from plate number twenty-eight of Asher Benjamin's book, *The Practice of Architecture*, written in 1833. He also wrote *Practical House Carpenter*. His designs were simple and were widely used in rural South Carolina during this era. Some of the other builders of this period had designs that were considerably more expensive to construct because they required more skilled labor.

The trim work on this house is very lovely and perfectly symmetrical. Built on a raised foundation, the house has four Ionic columns across the front of the pedimented portico, and Ionic pilasters at each end of the home. The door sidelights have a diamond-circle design flanked by pilasters. There is a double Greek fanlight above the door and above the window on each side of the front entrance. The windows are also framed by sidelights. The house is white frame with a hip roof. The woodwork and the chimneys are said to be the work of Badgett, who was an architect. The bricks used in the foundation and chimneys were made in his brickyard, located on the bank of a small stream that flowed in front of the house. There is a twelve-foot ceiling in the center hallway and the front rooms but not as high in the back rooms.

Badgett came to Laurens from Virginia before 1846. He was the builder of the Episcopal church and, also, a small building that is now used as a dental office. A daughter, Susan Dona, inherited the house. She was married to William James Copeland. When William's estate was settled, the property was bought by Alsey Copeland. Dr. Rossie Walker, the next owner, never lived in the home. The property was purchased from him by Mr. and Mrs. Ezell Garrett; it has recently been purchased and restored.

The house is located on the left side of Highway 49 just after leaving the city limits of Laurens. It is a perfectly balanced gem of a house. Even though it is not open to the public, it is easily viewed from the highway.

OCTAGON HOUSE

East Main Street

Zelotes Lee Holmes, a Presbyterian minister, came from New York to South Carolina in 1840. He was a professor of mathematics and philosophy at Laurens Female College. His land was surveyed in 1857, and construction on his home was begun in 1858. It was completed late in 1859, but the family moved in and occupied a few rooms prior to the completion.

The walls are twelve to eighteen inches thick, and the house rests on five-feet-high slabs made of large granite rocks and a concrete-like mortar. The home's exterior is stucco and scored to resemble stone. The octagon-shaped house was probably inspired by Orson Squire Fowler. The Capt. James Frazier House of Cedar Springs, S.C. is also octagon shaped and likely used Fowler's design. This shape, used primarily in building barns, schools, and churches, was less popular in the South than in other areas of the country. There are a few in Virginia, North Carolina, Georgia, Alabama, and Mississippi. Fowler was convinced that this type of construction was much less expensive than others.

While Fowler's design probably inspired Holmes, he seems to have copied a plan from Samuel Sloan's *The Model Architect* (1852). The plan has four corner rooms, four porches, and a central hall, the ceiling of which rises thirty-five feet and is topped by a skylight. The woodwork moldings are very beautiful. There are sixteen chimneys of various heights, and they are arranged in such a manner as to make the top of the house and roof line very striking indeed.

After the death of Reverend Holmes, his wife, daughter Ada, and her husband, Dr. L. S. Fowler, continued to live in the house. The Guy Watson family and then Mrs. Theodore Sumeral were the subsequent owners of the home. The house is currently unoccupied and is in a very sad state of disrepair. The citizens of Laurens have tried unsuccessfully to secure funds to restore this outstanding property. Hopefully, the house will be saved.

JESSIE HIX HOUSE

612 South Harper Street

Two brothers, Jessie Scott Hix and Edward Hix, came from Virginia to Union and then on to Laurens in the 1850s. Jessie built a house on South Harper Street. The home still stands on its original site and is one of the oldest houses in Laurens. Mrs. H. S. Blackwell later owned the house. Edward's home was on West Main Street and was replaced by the First United Methodist Church. The third brother, Press Hix, was an artist and lived in New York. His paintings are still highly valued by his descendants. Jessie and Edward operated a gristmill on the bank of Hix Creek, and they also operated a furniture factory.

The white frame cottage of Williamsburg design has three dormers with windows of six over six. There are two windows of six over six on each side of the front entry, which has double doors with sidelights and a double transom. The home rests on a brick foundation. A small wing is slightly recessed from the main house and has a separate entrance. The high-pitched roof is seamed metal. The present owners are restoring the home. It is not open to the public.

WILLIAMS-DUNKLIN HOUSE

West Main Street and
Dunklin Lane

The Dunklin House is one of the oldest in Laurens. It was constructed in 1812 by Washington Williams for his daughter and her husband. In 1843 Samuel Todd, a physician, purchased the property.

It has been described as a simplified Georgian or an upcountry farmhouse. The clapboard exterior is heart pine. The symmetrical arrangement of the windows and door was typical of the nineteenth century in upstate South Carolina. Windows are nine over nine and contain the original glass. Six square columns support the roof of the porch which extends across the front. There are four chimneys; two are "pipestems," which is unusual for the state.

The floor plan has remained basically unchanged, with two rooms on each side of a central hall. The ceilings are eleven feet high. The two front rooms have the original mantels with fluted pilasters. Two large, upstairs bedrooms have mantels identical to the ones on the first floor.

A slave cabin, a reconstructed Colonial Williamsburg-style kitchen, and small apartments are located behind the home. It is a house museum featuring a fine collection of Southern antiques, and is open to the public. There is an admission charge.

GOVERNOR SIMPSON HOUSE

West Main Street

Christopher Garlington designed and constructed this mansion. He probably used one of the pattern books available for assistance in the design phase—this was a common practice. The Greek Revival home was built in 1839. John Adam Eichelberger used the home as a town house when it came into his possession; William Dunlap Simpson purchased it from him at the end of the War Between the States. Simpson was a graduate of South Carolina College (University of South Carolina) and Harvard Law School. He had been a member of the South Carolina House of Representatives and was a state senator when the state seceded from the Union. When the war was over he was elected to serve in the United States House of Representatives, but because of having served as a lieutenant colonel in the army of the Confederacy he was refused his seat.

Simpson served as lieutenant governor in 1876 with Gov. Wade Hampton. In 1879, Simpson became governor when Hampton was elected United States senator and was appointed chief justice of the South Carolina Supreme Court.

A series of brick steps lead the way to the impressive three-story white frame house, where two pairs of Doric columns support a pediment. The six-over-six windows feature pilasters and sidelights. There is wood carving above the windows and door. The roof is gabled, and there are four chimneys.

On the first and second floors there are five rooms; the third floor has one large room that was used for large parties and balls. The rooms have unusual doors that rise when opened in order to clear the rugs. All of the rooms are quite large. The mantels are Greek Revival, and the fireplaces now burn coal rather than wood. All the floors are pine.

Some changes have been made to accommodate modern conveniences, but the exterior is virtually unchanged. This is a private residence.

Clinton

The small city of Clinton is located in Laurens County. People of this city have had a long history of compassionate responses to human need. In 1874, seeing the needs of orphan children, the Thornwell Home for Children was begun and occupied one stone building. It is the third oldest Presbyterian institution of this kind in the United States.

Before 1880 Dr. William States Jacobs founded Clinton College, which later became Presbyterian College. At first the academic offerings were on the high school level. Today the school offers a highly respected educational experience at the college level.

Whitten Village, a state-owned institution for the mentally retarded, is likewise located in Clinton.

There are many lovely residences and church buildings situated on impressive tree-lined streets. The city is a place of cultural and educational activities.

RANDOLPH LITTLE HOUSE
600 North Broad Street

The date established for the building of this lovely house is 1862. Randolph Little built the house with beams of solid heart pine. The first-level floors are oak, and the second-level floors are pine. During one period of its history a hall connected the front and back porches. The ceilings are of pinewood. The windows on both levels are six over six, and twin brick chimneys at each end frame the house. The home has had modern conveniences installed including a modern kitchen.

Local postmaster, "Press" Little, inherited the house. In 1909 Mrs. B. F. Godfrey purchased it and her son, Ansel, inherited it from her. Mr. Godfrey sold it in 1944 to Sterling Young, a member of the staff at Presbyterian College. The G. C. McInvailes purchased the house in 1952. Beautiful flowers and towering trees around this white frame home indicate loving care by the present owners.

The house is private.

R. N. S. YOUNG HOUSE

508 South Broad Street

Robert Newton Spires Young built the house on South Broad Street in 1848. It is possible that this may be the oldest house in Clinton. There is another house of questionable construction date which may predate the Young house.

Young donated land for the location of a new college. He made one unusual request as he presented the land: he asked that the front of the college would face his home. Some reports state that the request actually was that the front door of the college would be in a perfect line with the front door of his home. There may be validity to this because to this day the front door of the administrative building of Presbyterian College is in a line with the front door of the Young house.

The house on South Broad was the birthplace of all the children of Robert and Nancy Stroud Young. Sarah Elizabeth Young married John Calhoun Copeland and inherited the house. Her daughter, Lana, married Dr. Jack Holland Young and became the owner of the house at the death of her mother. Her daughter, Elizabeth Young Dick, inherited the home from her mother and in turn deeded the property to her daughter, Lana Copeland Dick. The house is unoccupied at this time.

Though the house needs repair, it is an elegant home. It is a two-story white frame with a porch gracing the front, upheld by six beautiful columns. There is a chimney at each end of the house. Windows upstairs and on each side of the entrance are flanked by sidelights. The front door has sidelights, a transom in three sections, and pilasters on each side of the sidelights that reflect the columns across the front. The home is not open to the public.

DAVIDSON HOUSE (MUSGROVE-OWENS)

513 Musgrove Street

This two-story white frame house was built in the 1820s. George Henry Davidson was the son of Capt. John Davidson of Charleston. He was the first citizen by the name of Davidson in Clinton's records. At the death of his mother, George made his home with relatives. He was an avid gardener and became a very fine furniture designer. A workshop was located behind his house in which he made some beautiful masterpieces still prized by members of his family.

This home remained in the Davidson family until 1942, when Thomas Richard Owens became the owner. His son, Thomas Richard Owens, is the present owner.

The single window of the main part of the house downstairs has sidelights as does the door. Over the door there is a transom. A porch extends across the front of the house on the lower level and is upheld by decorative columns.

The small room at the side is said to have been used as a schoolroom, probably the first in Clinton.

This is a private dwelling.

FERGERSON-DEAN-DAVENPORT HOUSE

707 Calvert Street

According to the South Carolina Department of History and Archives the Fergerson House was completed in 1850. There is a conflicting report, however, which cites an earlier date. The builder was George Madison Fergerson, and he, Mrs. Fergerson, and some of the children are buried in the Clinton Cemetery. The Russell Deans bought the house from the Joe Leake estate and moved it to its present location. Mr. and Mrs. Cecil Davenport purchased the house from the Deans and are in the process of completing extensive restoration.

The house is a Greek Revival cottage with a seam-metal hip roof and is put together with pegs. There are octagonal panels both horizontal and vertical across the front of the house, and the columns on the front portico are also octagonal. This octagonal design is carried throughout the house in the paneling on the doors. The original double front doors had been replaced with one door. One of these walnut doors was discovered in a pantry. The Deans had it reproduced and once again installed the double doors. Many of the panes of glass in the sidelights on each side of the front doors are of the original handblown glass.

Heart-pine doors are used in the entrance hall. The corner moldings are unusual (almost rare). Apparently there was originally a room on each side of the entrance hall. The fireplaces were interior and could not be saved when the house was moved, so bathrooms were installed in these areas.

Although this is a small cottage, the twelve-foot ceilings with their hand-cut boards create an air of spaciousness.

A modern living area including kitchen and family rooms has been added to the rear of the house. It is not visible from the front. The original kitchen was separated from the house and is located in the backyard. The present owners have plans for connecting this with a guest area.

It is not possible adequately to describe this charming cottage. The architectural features on the front of the house are unique and must be seen to be appreciated.

OLD NINETY-SIX DISTRICT

Greenwood

Provincial governor James Glen purchased land from the Cherokee Indians in 1747 which included all of their land south and east of Long Cane Creek. Government was centralized in Charleston. In 1767 the province was divided into six judicial districts; one of those was Ninety-Six District. Included in that territory were the present counties of Spartanburg, Newberry, Union, Laurens, Abbeville, and Edgefield. The town of Ninety-Six, the judicial seat, was mentioned on a map made in 1730 by George Hunter. Its location was ninety-six miles from Keowee, which was at that time the largest Cherokee Indian settlement. The early settlers of the district were English, Scotch, Scotch-Irish, German, and French Huguenots. They were devoutly religious people.

The first southern land battle of the Revolutionary War was fought at the town of Ninety-Six. In 1790 the British captured the town, but Gen. Nathanael Greene besieged the British troops. It was a long and bitter struggle, during which the Torries burned and pillaged the area. The battlefield is a national park and is open to visitors.

Old Ninety-Six historic sites may be seen in Edgefield County, McCormick County, Abbeville County, and Greenwood County. There are many beautiful and historic homes in the area.

Originally Greenwood County was a part of Abbeville and Edgefield counties. Although there were settlers in Greenwood by 1750, the county was not formed until 1897. The settlers were farmers and primarily English speaking.

VANCE-MAXWELL HOUSE

158 East Cambridge Street

The Vance-Maxwell House is thought to have been built in 1850 for Allen Vance, the son of Nathaniel and Mary McTier Vance. The most prominent owner was Dr. John C. Maxwell, who owned the home from 1871 to 1879. During the War Between the States Maxwell, then a resident of Abbeville County, enrolled in Captain Perryman's "Secession Guards" and became the regimental surgeon. In 1876 he was elected to the Senate in the South Carolina General Assembly, in which capacity he served for nine years. He was associated with Wade Hampton and, also, assumed a very active leadership role in the organization of Greenwood County. He served on a number of important committees and was very active in civic affairs in Greenwood.

Dr. Maxwell and his wife, Sally Richardson Maxwell, had five children. None lived past infancy except Connie, who lived to be eight years old. In 1891 Dr. and Mrs. Maxwell promised a gift of 470 acres to help establish a Baptist orphanage, which would be named in memory of this child. Since that time the Connie Maxwell Children's Home has cared for more than six thousand children. Dr. Maxwell died in 1899 and Mrs. Maxwell in 1902, at which time the Vance-Maxwell House became the property of the Connie Maxwell Children's Home. George Neel bought the home in 1903.

Originally built as a one and one-half story farmhouse, it was remodeled between 1898 and 1904 in the Second Empire style. A full second floor was added at this time. A one-story porch extends across the front of the main part of the house. The roof has three quite steep gablets, with small arched windows in each. The front entry is also arched. Early in the twentieth century, one-story wings were added at each end of the house. The kitchen building dating to 1856 has been added to the rear of the main house. The central hall plan with rooms on each side was used on both levels.

The home is privately owned.

THE MOORE HOUSE

426 Reynolds Street

William Judge Moore was born in 1857. His wife was the former Connie Amelia Elleson. The first Master in Equity in Greenwood County, Mr. Moore was an attorney, a farmer, and served several terms in the state legislature.

This "picture book" Victorian house was built in the late 1800s by the Moores. The trim on the house is very ornate. There are three different siding finishes on this three-story white frame house. There is a turret on one side and high peaked gable on the other. Notice the sunburst on each side of the windows on the third floor of the gable. The twin chimneys are most unusual. The windows are single pane over single, and the windows under the eaves of the wrap-around porch are quite large with transoms. There is also a transom over the front entrance.

This home is privately owned.

BARRATT HOUSE

Highway 67 South

The Barratt House is a two-story English-Gothic Revival stuccoed building. It was designed and built by Dr. John P. Barratt about 1853-56 for his son, John Joseph. Dr. Barratt was born in 1795 in Wakefield, Yorkshire, England. He came to the United States in 1816 and taught school in Edgefield. After a few years he attended New York College of Physicians and Surgeons. He returned to South Carolina to practice medicine and married Mrs. Lavina Brooks Watson, who had inherited a plantation from her first husband. She and Barratt lived in the home until 1859. Mrs. Barratt had four children; she and Barratt had a daughter and a son. Dr. Barratt began a school to educate his children and others in the area. He was an inventor, a naturalist, an educator as well as a scientist and physician.

The home was originally a square building with a gable roof of seamed metal. The front and rear of the house are identical and divided by three bays with steep gables. The windows are six over six, flanked by two over two and crowned with arched pediments. The front entrance is recessed and has a Gothic archivolt made up of three arches. Wings were added at a later date, and great care was exercised to ensure their compatibility with the rest of the house. A central hall with four large rooms on each level is the plan by which the original house was arranged. Wood carvings which grace the interior were made by Dr. Barratt. Mr. and Mrs. T. E. Dorn purchased the property and lived there for many years. Subsequently, their son, former congressman W. J. Bryan Dorn, bought the property. Congressman and Mrs. Dorn restored the home and furnished it in the style of the period.

This is a private residence.

Abbeville

Abbeville was founded in 1758. It was named for a city in France which was the hometown of Dr. John de la Howe, an outstanding French Huguenot settler of the area. Abbeville is located in the western South Carolina hills in Abbeville County. The town grew up around the home of Gen. Andrew Pickens. Another famous statesman, John C. Calhoun, was born here.

A large section of Abbeville is a National Historic District. There are many interesting and beautiful old homes and churches in the city, the center of which has been restored to its former glory. The opera house has been reopened and features outstanding theatrical productions.

Some consider this the "birthplace" and the "deathbed" of the Confederacy. In 1860 an assembly voted to leave the Union and in 1865 Confederate president Jefferson Davis had his last council of war meeting in the home now known as the Burt-Stark House.

A map of Historic Abbeville is available with additional information. Call (803) 459-4600.

QUAY-WARDLAW HOUSE

104 Church Street

Quay-Wardlaw House is probably the oldest house in the Abbeville Historic District. It was erected of log and frame construction about 1786 to 1790. There were four or five houses built in the district during this time period, but this is the only one remaining.

Archival records indicate that the Church Street entrance was not always the main one. The other entrance to this one and one-half story house featured three bays with the entrance in the center. The first-floor windows are nine over nine, and the second-story windows are six over nine. The entrance from Church Street has a one-story side porch and a gabled wing with a boxed cornice. The chimney has unusual brick. Some of the rows are made of very small brick, and some are made of average-sized brick but there seems to be no pattern for the use of the different sizes. The core of the house is a two-story log building. Currently, the house is painted blue with white trim.

Available records do not reveal information about the builder or the subsequent occupants through the years.

The house is private.

OLD HOMES OF SOUTH CAROLINA

BURT-STARK HOUSE

Intersection of Greenville and Main

This two-story white frame house with lap siding was designed by David Lesley for Armistead Burt in about 1830. Burt married Martha Calhoun in 1828. The house remained in the Burt family until 1971, when Mary Stark Davis gave it and all its furnishings to the Abbeville Historic Preservation Commission.

Four square columns support the pedimented front portico. Beneath the pediment is a small second-story balcony trimmed with latticework. Latticework also embellishes the two small porches at each end of the house. Floor-length windows on each side of the front door open onto the main portico.

The house features high ceilings, heart-pine flooring, and ceiling medallions. On each side of the large central hall there are drawing rooms closed by double doors. When these were opened, a large ballroom was created.

The historic marker in front of the house indicates that when Jefferson Davis left Richmond after its fall in 1865, he traveled south in an effort to rally his forces. He, along with his cabinet, spent the night in this house, the home of his good friend, Maj. Armistead Burt. It was here that the decision was made to "abandon all hope" and just to try to get President Davis safely away in his escape to the west. The meeting was cited as his last council of war.

Contact the Abbeville Historic Commission for information regarding visits to the house.

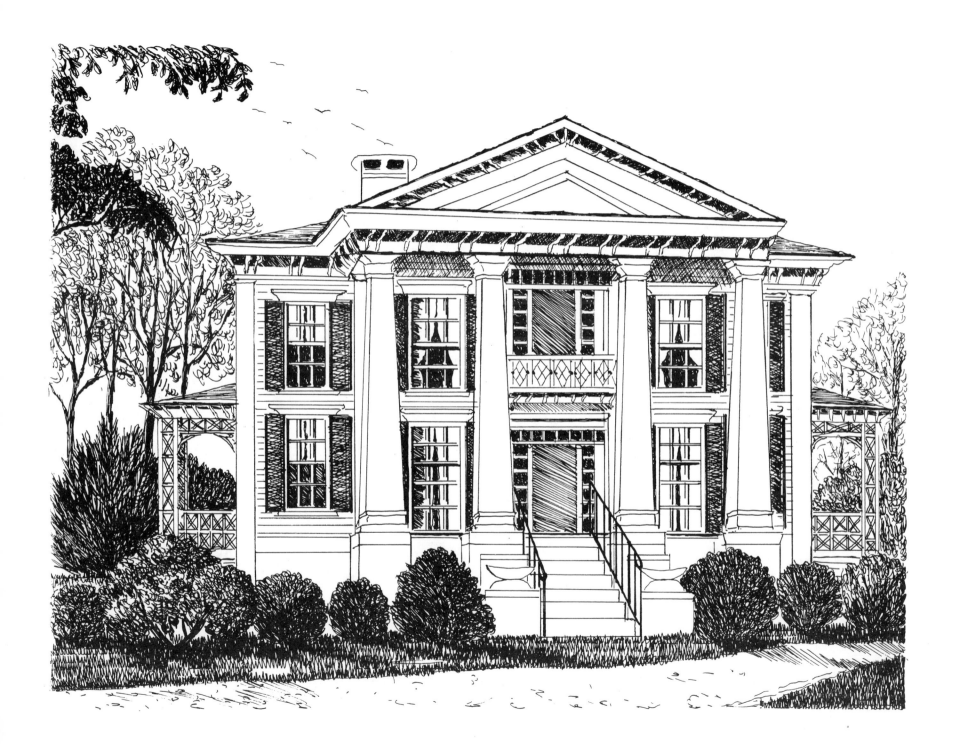

McCormick

McCormick County was originally in the old Ninety-Six District. The term "district" was changed in 1868 and the counties were organized. Several counties that came into existence at that time were later divided to form new counties. A small part from each of Abbeville, Greenwood, and Edgefield counties was taken to form McCormick County in 1916.

The first inhabitants of the area were the Cherokee Indians. The Cherokee War took place at Long Cane Settlement in 1760 and became known as the Long Cane Massacre.

Fort Charlotte, located on the Savannah River, was founded by the English Crown in 1765. It was the first fort seized by the American troops at the beginning of the Revolutionary War.

In 1852 William B. Dorn discovered the second richest vein of gold in the state at Peak's Hill. It was soon the largest mine in South Carolina and one of the richest in the United States.

The name "McCormick" was chosen to honor Cyrus McCormick, the inventor of the reaper. He bought the gold mine from Mr. Dorn but never lived in the county.

Several historic sites in the county provide interesting stops for the visitor.

IVY GATES

State Highway 38

Henry Jones, who built Eden Hall, Long Cane Church, and the Calhoun House, was the builder for Ivy Gates. The construction took about two years and was completed in 1856.

The house was built for Dr. Moses A. T. Wideman and remained in the Wideman family until 1979, when it was purchased by Howard and Judy Clayton. The Wideman family was from Germany. Miss Jennie Wideman and her servant, Josie, were the last of the family actually to live there. At Jennie's death, the house was left to her brother, Boyce, of Columbia. It was subsequently inherited by his children.

The Claytons have been restoring the home and furnishing it with antiques. Mrs. Clayton says that the beautiful hand-carved staircase is still very sound. This carving was supervised by Jones, the architect.

Ivy Gates is a two-story white frame house on a raised basement. It also has an attic. The style seems to be representative of the Federal era with a small portico on the front. There are two square columns and two engaged columns. The door opening onto the small upstairs porch has sidelights and a transom. The main entrance features a double door, also with sidelights and a transom. The upstairs windows are nine over six and those downstairs are nine over nine. The windows are flanked by very unusual shutters. There are ten rooms, three baths, and six porches. Huge trees surround the house, and the gate is encircled with ivy.

The house is located approximately midway between Abbeville and McCormick just across the McCormick County line. It is at the intersection of Highways 38 and 117. Off of Highway 28 turn left at the crest of the hill beyond the Troy historical marker.

This is a private home.

OLD PENDLETON DISTRICT

Anderson

Anderson, Oconee, and Pickens counties originally constituted the Pendleton District. Pendleton was the "courthouse town," but a new and more centrally located place was needed for this purpose. Col. Robert Anderson was the founder of the Pendleton District, and the town named in his honor was chosen for the new "courthouse town." Here, in 1890, William C. Whitner invented the means by which electricity was transmitted for a distance. Anderson is still referred to as "the electric city." This city had the first cotton mill in the South and the first cotton gin to be powered by electricity. One of the first cities in the nation to have streetcars was Anderson. Today it is the center for many diversified industries. Lake Hartwell is immediately adjacent to the city and accommodates all types of water sports. The climate is such that it has attracted many individuals from other areas of the nation to make it their home. In the spring the city is a veritable garden with a profusion of azaleas and dogwoods.

Some of the most impressive homes in the state may be found in this county, four of which are very unusual. Dr. Harold Cooledge, professor emeritus of architecture at Clemson University, coined a descriptive architectural term in referring to these homes. He identified them as Chinese Chippendale because of the pagoda roof line. The houses have tall pointed gables, and the roof lines slope inward.

Cooledge said that there were only five of these in the country, and four were in Anderson. The other is in Charleston. Cooledge said this style is related to a type of architecture used in the nineteenth century for the eastern shore. Sometimes it is referred to as the "stick style," Queen Anne Revival, or Gothic Revival.

One of the four houses, the John Sullivan House on McDuffie Street, was built in 1858 and has been unoccupied for years. During that time it has deteriorated badly. It is said to be the birthplace of George Bell Timmerman, Jr., former governor of the state.

Other houses of this type are the Hubbard-McFall-King House, the Wilhite-Geisberg House, and the Clinkscales Home. Callie Rainey (Mrs. John Rainey) is perhaps the person most instrumental in preserving the lovely old homes of the city. She would purchase a house, paint it, and restore it to a point where it could be occupied. Then she would either rent it or sell it to one who would take care of it and love it. These old homes are a testimony to Callie Rainey's true interest in historic preservation.

THE CALDWELL-JOHNSON-MORRIS HOUSE

Morris Street

In 1846, James J. Caldwell, a native of Newberry, was elected to the Chancery bench and later became circuit solicitor. His widow, Nancy, moved to Anderson to be near her children who were in school there and in Pendleton. She purchased four acres of land and built a "colonial cottage" (also called "raised cottage"). This type of construction was very common in the Midlands.

In 1853 the home was sold to Dr. William Bullein Johnson for the sum of $3,800 following the death of Mrs. Caldwell. Johnson had gone to Anderson to become president of a female seminary which was named in his honor. In the fifth year Johnson suggested that the school be given university status.

Johnson was an attorney and a graduate of Brown University. After attending a revival service at the Baptist Church of Beaufort, he felt called by God to enter the ministry. He served as pastor of several churches in the low country of South Carolina.

As a chaplain of South Carolina College (which later became the University of South Carolina), Johnson organized the First Baptist Church of Columbia in 1809. In 1831 he organized the First Baptist Church of Greenville.When the Triennial Baptist Convention, of which Johnson was president, voted to form a Southern Baptist Convention, he was its first president.

At his death in 1862 his casket, preceded by the university students, was carried from his home to Anderson's First Baptist Church. His remains were interred in the cemetery at the church.

Miss Margaret Morris became the new owner of the home. Her sister, Elizabeth Primrose Morris, taught school and a music class there. These sisters lived in the house for more than fifty years.

Mrs. John Rainey (Callie) was instrumental in restoring this cottage. The grounds are a "swept" garden which was typical of the period. It is now a tearoom. Manning Street divides at Morris Street, and the home faces north on Manning. It is white frame with a full basement and high steps leading to the entry on the main floor.

CLINKSCALES HOME

Highway 252

The Clinkscales Home is located on Highway 252 just off of the Belton Highway between Anderson and Honea Path. It is Chinese Chippendale and was constructed more than one hundred years ago. The design was probably from a pattern book which was available to anyone who desired to use it. The sparkling white frame house is perfectly balanced with two very tall pagoda-type gables in the front with a smaller gable between. The bargeboard is very ornate. The roofs of the side dormers are also pagoda-shaped with an inward slant. Slender round columns with very elaborately carved capitals uphold the sloped roof of the porch. Windows are six over six with a curved triangular pediment and are flanked by shutters. The molding on the front door is outlined in a dark color which is almost black. There are delicate sidelights and transom lights.

An Anderson architect says that the house is Steamboat Gothic, which is similar to Chinese Chippendale. However, Dr. Cooledge, emeritus professor of architecture at Clemson University, labeled it Chinese Chippendale. The Hubbard-McFall-King House resembles Steamboat Gothic much more than does this one.

Bill Clinkscales, the present owner, was born in the house in 1904. He and his family have been very influential in the area for many years. His mother was Selma Wright Clinkscales. Her father, husband, son, two sons-in-law, and two grandsons were all members of the South Carolina legislature. Bill was elected a member of the General Assembly nine times.

This house is privately owned and not open to the public.

WILHITE-GEISBERG HOUSE

514 South McDuffie Street

The Wilhite-Geisberg House is one of Anderson's four Chinese Chippendale homes. The influence is not as pronounced in this home as in the other three, but it does feature a pagoda-type roof. This house was built about 1882 by Frank T. Wilhite, son of Dr. and Mrs. Phillip Wilhite. It was the early home of another of their sons and his bride. Later, Mr. and Mrs. Oscar Geisberg of Vienna, Austria, purchased the home. Mr. Geisberg went to Anderson as a part of the Federal occupation troops following the War Between the States. The couple remained in Anderson, and he became a well-respected businessman. He organized the Board of Trade, which was the forerunner of the Chamber of Commerce, and was also instrumental in the organization of the YMCA.

The building now houses a law office.

THE HUBBARD-MCFALL-KING HOUSE

518 Evans Street

According to an Anderson legend, John Hubbard and his new wife, Lavina Cater Hubbard, took a honeymoon trip to New York during which time she saw a house on the banks of the Hudson River and was captivated by it. John sketched it, and when they returned he built a very similar house for his bride. It was completed in 1893 and is Chinese Chippendale style. Some refer to it as "the house of many gables." The builder was Alexander Towers Skelton. Painted a soft grey, it has white trim with "gingerbread" woodwork. The barge-board or gableboard is joined near the peak of the gable with an ornate frame cross. Slender round columns support the roof of the porch that almost encircles the house. Although there are only six rooms in this one-story house, it feels quite spacious because of a large central hall and ceilings throughout that are sixteen feet high. The fireplaces are enamel-faced. The floors are heart pine except for the hallway, which has inlaid walnut.

The present owners are Stanley and Kelley King. Stanley is the great-grandson of the John Hubbards. Their grand-daughter, Joan McFall, and her husband, Wilbur King, are the parents of Stanley. Stanley's daughter, Leigh, is the fifth generation to live in this beautiful old home.

The home is not open to the public.

THE ORR-BUTLER-STONE HOUSE

407 South Manning Street

Christopher Orr's Tavern, as it was known, was built in approximately 1835. It is probably the oldest house remaining in Anderson on which few changes have been made. It was built by Christopher Orr, the son of Gov. James L. Orr, who was the first governor elected by the people after the War Between the States. The home was originally on South Main Street and was a tavern in the early days of Anderson history. It is a frame home set on a raised basement and was the first of its kind in the city. There is a small porch with four square posts upholding the triangular pediment. On the second level, a central window opens onto a small balcony trimmed with wrought iron. The windows have the original handblown glass. The doors appear to have been put together with pegs. The large front door has sidelights and a transom.

This is a private home.

Pendleton District

Pendleton District included what is now Anderson, Oconee, and Pickens counties. This area was a part of the Great Cherokee Nation in which the Cherokee Indians lived long before the Europeans arrived. In 1753 the English built Fort Prince George to protect the Cherokee from the Creek Indians. More than incidentally, it would protect the English, also. During the Revolution the Cherokees were loyal to the English. Later, they ceded to the state of South Carolina the land area included in the three counties mentioned above plus Greenville County. The district was named Pendleton in honor of Judge Henry Pendleton of Virginia.

A courthouse was established in 1790. In 1826 the legislature divided the district into Anderson and Pickens districts. Oconee County was a part of Pickens District when the counties were set up in 1868.

LOWTHER HALL

161 East Queen Street

Tradition has it that Lowther Hall is the oldest house in the town of Pendleton. Early records provide conflicting information with regard to Lord Lowther's relationship to this property. One cannot be certain whether or not the Englishman built the house as a hunting lodge or ever even owned the place. It was originally built of logs using massive, solid tree trunks. The logs were fastened in place with foot-long oak pegs. Archival records indicate that in 1793 William Hunter purchased lots on which he erected a house, kitchen, and other buildings. In 1805, Robert Anderson, Jr., serving as a trustee for William Shaw, purchased the place. It seems that William Bradfoot purchased part of the property for Lord Lowther in 1816. Tolly Bowling of Greenville bought the house known as "Lowther Hall" in 1838, and in 1852 the Pendleton Lodge, Ancient Free Masons, bought the place.

William Henry Trescot, a diplomat and an author, acquired the home in 1895, and it was enlarged to its present size. At one time he was appointed secretary to the American legation in London. In 1860, he became assistant secretary of state as a result of an appointment by President Buchanan. He served on a special commission regulating Chinese immigration into the United States. He also served as a special envoy to Chile, Peru, and Bolivia. Before he died in this home in 1898, he had also worked on negotiations for a treaty with Mexico.

Years after the Trescot addition to the house, a bedroom was changed into the kitchen. All of the floors are original with the exception of the dining room. This beautiful two-story white frame home has recently been restored. It has a one-story verandah with Tuscan columns supporting the shed roof of the porch. The windows upstairs are nine over nine, but the ones downstairs are much larger with twelve over twelve. There are two front doors, each of which has sidelights and a transom. The house is on a raised basement and has a hip roof.

This is a private residence.

ELAM SHARPE HOUSE

229 East Queen

The traditional date accepted for the construction of this home is 1802, but there is no confirming evidence to support this date. On December 13, 1818, Elam Sharpe purchased one-half of lot number forty-four from John Miller. It is assumed that printer John Miller built the home. At the time of the purchase records made no mention of a house, but in 1823 the executors of William Steele's estate sold a lot to John Miller, and those records reveal that Sharpe lived on the adjacent lot.

William Sharpe and Catherine Reese Sharpe were the parents of Elam. His uncle was Dr. Thomas Reese, the first pastor of Hopewell-on-the-Keewee. William was a lawyer and a member of the Continental Congress in Philadelphia. Elam married Elizabeth, John Miller's granddaughter, and they had five children. Elam Jr. married the daughter of Gov. Robert Hayne.

This home was built of heart-pine boards that were hand-sawed. The exposed overhead beams were also hand-sawed. There is an entrance hall between the two downstairs rooms, and two rooms across the back under a shed roof. The upstairs hall, reached by a curved stairway from the downstairs hall, has one room on each side. Each room features the original mantel and fireplace. Windows upstairs are nine over six, and the central window is larger with sidelights. The downstairs windows are nine over nine. Double stairs lead from the yard to the small entrance porch. The front door has sidelights and a fan-shaped transom.

This is a private home.

BOXWOOD

237 East Queen Street

William Robertson (or Robinson) bought town lots forty-six and forty-seven in 1809. When he sold two acres in 1811, indications are that a house was on the land. Successive owners of the house were as follows: Joab Mauldin, J. B. Earle, Joseph Grisham, E. B. Benson, J. V. Shanklin, and John T. Sloan. Mr. and Mrs. Harlan McClune remodeled and restored the house in 1959-60. Mr. McClune was the dean of the College of Architecture of Clemson University. His research indicates that there were additions made to the house in 1825 and 1835.

Boxwood is a two-story frame house with a one-tier porch across the front. Houses of the period commonly had four or six posts or columns across the front supporting porches, but this house is unusual in that it has seven posts. The chimneys at each end of the house have a unique brick pattern. One of the downstairs windows is very large and is flanked by double-wide shutters. Wooden carvings on the pilasters of the front door are very fine examples of that art. The door has sidelights and a transom.

Many boxwoods that are believed to be over 150 years old grow on the property, hence the home's name.

This is a private dwelling.

SIMPSON HOUSE

215 North Elm Street

F. Frank Sloan was the first occupant of this house built in 1830 by Jessie P. Lewis. The raised two-story house has a hip roof and is flanked by two chimneys. Square posts support the roof of the one-story porch, with arched latticework between the posts. On each side of the upstairs windows are unusual pierced shutters.

Richard F. and Margaret Taliaferro Simpson were the parents of Richard Wright Simpson. He was born on the family farm. Richard was a senior at Wofford College when war was begun at Fort Sumter in 1861. He served as a private in Company A, Third Regiment of the South Carolina Volunteers. In 1874 he was elected to the state legislature. He also served on Gov. Wade Hampton's staff.

The changes that were brought about by war convinced Mr. Simpson that education was vitally important to rebuilding the South. He worked with Thomas Clemson as his confidential advisor and was very interested in seeing an agricultural college established. He wrote Clemson's will and was the executor of the estate which made the agricultural college possible. His was an obviously strong influence in the founding of Clemson University. He was the chairman of the board of trustees of the college.

Simpson inherited his parents' farm, but spent most of his time in this home in Pendleton where he practiced law.

This is a private home.

WOODBURN PLANTATION

U.S. Highway 76 and
S.C. Highway 279

Charles Cotesworth Pinckney was born in 1789 while his father, Thomas Pinckney, was governor of South Carolina. Charles built Woodburn in 1858. He was a member of the Nullification Convention in 1832 and became lieutenant governor in 1833. He was an alumnus of Harvard University. In spite of the fact that he had studied law, he became a planter with as much as two thousand acres of rice under cultivation on several plantations. His father was an influential scientific agriculturalist.

Dr. John B. Adger, minister and missionary, bought the home in the 1850s and enlarged it. The next owner was a nephew, Augustus Smythe of Charleston. He created a stock farm and raised racehorses and purebred cattle.

Woodburn is a white frame house with rooms on four levels. The two-story verandahs wrap around each side of the building. The carved Doric columns on both levels are quite large. The windows and doors extend from the floor to the ceiling.

The house is operated by the Pendleton District Historical and Recreation Commission and is open to the public. There is an admission charge.

Oconee

From the foothills to the mountain peaks, Oconee is one of the most beautiful counties in the state. Its beginnings go back to the Cherokee Indians and many places still bear the Indian names. It is located in the northwest corner of the state with the Chattooga National Wild and Scenic River serving as the boundary between South Carolina and Georgia. The mountains to the north provide a border between North Carolina and South Carolina. Whitewater Falls, the highest falls east of the Mississippi River, are just north of the state line.

Lake Jocassee, Lake Keowee, and many streams with headwaters in the mountains offer fishing, boating, and other sporting adventures. Oconee State Park has cottages and camping facilities. One would be well advised to enjoy the scenic beauty of the drive across the Cherokee Foothills Highway 11.

The area around Walhalla, Westminster, and Seneca is known for the apple orchards which spread across acres and acres. The Apple Festival is a popular event each fall. This is a good time to purchase some of the apples grown in the area and to sample some of the delicious apple dishes for which the local cooks are famous.

WHETSTONE PLACE

Mountain Rest

On the way to Earl's Fort, beside Whetstone Road stands an old house that was built about 1835. In the early nineteenth century, Indians traveled this road to trade with the settlers and with those crossing over the river into Georgia. Earl's Fort is now where tourists go to try the "white water" rafting on the Chatooga River.

An itinerant builder with a team of slaves traveled from one settlement to another from 1830 to 1850 building homes. All of the houses were about the same design: two floors with a gallery across the front on the lower level. Each of the slaves was a specialist in carpentry or brick masonry. There are very few of these homes still in existence. The original owner of the Whetstone Place was Fidel Crisp. A surveyor, Edward Crisp, drew a plan of Charleston in 1704 as can be seen in a lithograph entitled "A Plan of Charles Town From a Survey of Edward Crisp, Esq. 1704." It is not known whether or not Fidel is a descendant of Edward.

The house soon passed into the hands of the Hamby family. In 1843 it was obtained by Abdel Robins, whose descendants still live in the community of Mountain Rest. Leroy Brown purchased the house and land in 1930. He farmed the land and rented the house. After a time, the house was empty and fell into disrepair. When the family considered destroying it, a grandson, Charles Moxley, expressed an interest in restoring the old home. His grandmother gave him the home, and he began work on the place in 1982. It was necessary to replace some of the flooring, but Moxley was able to obtain pine flooring of about the same vintage. He has been very faithful in maintaining the integrity of the restoration.

The interior walls are of eleven-inch-wide heart-pine boards. The only walls that are painted are the ones that were originally painted. The parlor is painted a soft white with Williamsburg Blue trim. Timbers are joined with pegs without nails. The chimneys are of handmade brick from horse-trampled mud. The bricks were made on the site, and one still bears the handprint of the mason who made it. The window sashes and glass on the first-floor level are original; in the front there are nine over nine while those in the back are nine over six. Upstairs the windows are six over nine. All of the mantels are of heart pine, hand-carved, and joined with pegs.

Mrs. Moxley (Kay), a professional interior designer, has decorated the home with lovely antiques and country designs. The whites and rich blue that she has used bring out the mellow tones of the old wood. There are four rooms downstairs—two on each side of a wide hallway. Upstairs there are two rooms.

A hand-dug well with nine feet of water standing in it is thought to have been dug by the original settlers. The Moxleys are constructing a log building directly behind the house which will provide rooms for bed and breakfast guests.

Whetstone Road intersects Highway 28 near Mountain Rest. Whetstone Place is approximately five miles from this intersection on the right side of the road. From the site one gets a beautiful view of the foothills and mountains.

Clemson

The city was originally named Calhoun. In 1943 the name was changed to Clemson, the name of the land-grant college which has become Clemson University. The town is centered around the school, the second largest in the state.

The Horticulture Greenhouse and Gardens have about two thousand varieties of plants. Clemson is highly recognized for its blue cheese.

John C. Calhoun, former vice-president of the United States, lived in Clemson. His home, Fort Hill, is now a house museum open to the public and is located on the university campus.

Hanover House is another historic home on the campus. It is a French Huguenot home that was moved from the low country. The cemetery by the Old Stone Church just out of Clemson is the burial place of Andrew Pickens.

Clemson is located in the southern edge of Pickens County on the shores of Lake Hartwell. The county extends up into the mountains to the North Carolina state line.

FORT HILL

Clemson University Campus

This mansion was built on land granted to Robert Tate in 1784. At that time this land parcel was named the Fort Hill Tract because of a fortification that was erected there in 1776. John Ewing Calhoun became the owner in the late 1700s. In 1802, Rev. James McElhenney obtained the land and built a very modest home which he named "Old Clergy Hall." There were four main rooms, two on the first floor and two on the second. The large fireplace, hearth, and the deep Dutch oven are still in the room at the right side of the entrance hall.

The estate was owned by Mrs. John Ewing Caldwell after McElhenney died. John Caldwell Calhoun married her daughter and later moved his family to Old Clergy Hall, which he rented from his mother-in-law. At the death of Mrs. Caldwell, Calhoun gained ownership of the property about 1836. He soon owned 1,100 acres.

Additions were made to the house as they were needed, and enlargement was necessary because the Calhouns had nine children. Mrs. Calhoun is reputed to have remodeled constantly, adding rooms until there were fourteen. The two-story white frame house has a large central portico with Tuscan columns and two-story porches on the east and south with plastered brick columns similar to those on the central portico.

The house was heated by fireplaces in every room, and each carved mantel was different from the others. The interior woodwork is red cedar.

On the west side of the original first floor are located the parlor, formal dining room, and family dining room. Almost all the bedrooms are on the second floor, and there are adjoining dressing rooms. Records indicate that the kitchen was probably not in the main part of the house.

John C. Calhoun was vice-president of the United States when he moved into this house in 1825. He had gained national recognition as secretary of war under James Monroe and later as secretary of state under John Tyler. Born in 1782 in Abbeville District, South Carolina, Calhoun graduated from Yale University in 1804 and studied law in South Carolina and Connecticut. He served in the South Carolina Legislature and the United States Senate.

After the death of Calhoun in 1850, his son-in-law, Thomas G. Clemson, inherited the property. Clemson made this his home for many years and bequeathed his estate to the state of South Carolina for the establishment of an agricultural and mechanical college. The will specified that the Calhoun Mansion, Fort Hill, shall never be torn down or altered.

With $80,000 and 814 acres from the Clemson estate, the college was founded in 1889 as a land grant college and named after the benefactor, Clemson.

Fort Hill is operated as a house museum and is open to the public.

HANOVER HOUSE

Clemson University Campus

Almost in ruins, the Hanover House faced certain destruction in the early 1940s when the waters of the Santee and Cooper rivers were to be used for a hydroelectric plant. Thomas Waterman, associate architect of the United States Department of the Interior, felt that this house was of national importance. The home was taken apart piece by piece, brick by brick, and each piece was numbered and labeled. It was then moved to the Clemson University campus. About 250 families assisted with the project.

Reading the history of this house is like reading a novel. It began a long time ago in Vitre, France. Protestants had enjoyed the right to worship as they chose for 100 years, but in 1671 they were ordered to close their temple. The princess of Tarente, a very devoted Protestant, had religious services for her family and friends in her own home, Chateau de Vitre. Among those attending these services were the Ravenels, the DuBourdieus, and the De St. Juliens. These Huguenots suffered a variety of persecutions, and eventually probably as many as fifty thousand of the Huguenots left France. In 1685 Pierre Julien de St. Julien, his wife, Jeanne LeFebvre, and nine children escaped to England. Rene Ravenel went with them. They arrived in South Carolina in 1686, and records show that Pierre Sr. received three 1,000-acre tracts granted by the lords proprietors.

Paul de St. Julien, grandson of Pierre, began building his home on one of these tracts of land in 1714. He named his home "Hanover" in appreciation for the kindnesses shown the Huguenots by the English following the revocation of the Edict of Nantes in 1685. George Lewis, elector of Hanover, became George I, king of England, that year.

Originally, Paul had planned a brick first floor, but he used so many bricks in the basement and the triple-flue chimney that his supply was exhausted. The walls of the basement were two feet thick. One can see in the mortar at the top of the chimney the words *Peu a Peu* from a longer French proverb which states: "Little by little the bird builds its nest."

Paul and his wife, Aimée Ravenel de St. Julien, moved into the house in late 1716. The house was quite different from the other plantation homes because it was very French in style. The roof is Gallic with dormers, and the doors are French. The shingles and siding are cypress. On the first floor are the drawing room, dining room, keeping room, and master's office. The second floor has four bedrooms. A family portrait, a French Huguenot Bible, and many other interesting items are displayed throughout the house.

When Paul de St. Julien died in 1741, his daughter, Mary, inherited Hanover. She married Henry Ravenel in 1750, and the home was identified with the Ravenels for 138 years. After his father's death, a son, Stephen, bought the plantation from his fifteen brothers and sisters. Stephen was a member of the South Carolina Legislature and also served as secretary of state.

Hanover belonged to several members of this family until 1904. Then James F. Taylor held title to the property from 1904 to 1905. There was a sizeable French Huguenot community in this area, and there is an active French Huguenot Church in Charleston today.

This home is a monument to the men and women who were determined to preserve their freedom to worship according to the dictates of their consciences even if it meant leaving their homes and all else that was dear to them.

The house is operated as a museum and is open to the public.

THE MIDLANDS

Columbia

As the state of South Carolina began to grow, the citizens from upstate requested that the site of the state capital be more centrally located. At that time Charleston was the capital.

The geographical center of the state was on the Congaree River. In 1749 John Taylor of Virginia had made his home in that area. Two of his sons had plantations on the site now known as Columbia. "Taylor's Hill" was chosen by the General Assembly for the new capital in 1786, and the name Columbia was agreed upon in honor of Christopher Columbus. The original area was two miles square and the streets were laid out in four-acre squares. In 1805, South Carolina College (later to become the University of South Carolina) opened for students.

There are several historic areas in the city featuring beautiful homes and public buildings. The South Carolina State Museum on Gervais Street is outstanding. It is a beautifully restored, four-story mill facility. The state Archives Building is also located in Columbia. There are regular tours through the State House (State Capitol building) and tours through the governor's mansion may be arranged. Several of the historic homes are operated as house museums and opened daily.

Riverbanks Zoological Park has been recognized with special awards for excellence. Several parks are in the downtown area. Lake Murray is one of the most beautiful lakes in the state and is located approximately twelve miles from the State House. For more information, contact: Greater Columbia Convention and Visitors' Bureau, 301 Gervais Street, Columbia, S.C. 29201, (803) 254-0479.

HAMPTON-PRESTON HOUSE

1615 Blanding Street

This stucco mansion was built in about 1818 by Ainsley Hall. Wade Hampton purchased it in 1823, and his daughter, Mrs. John S. Preston, inherited it. The home was occupied by Union general J. A. Logan and became his headquarters during the Reconstruction period (1872-74). For the next forty-one years, the Hampton-Preston House was the location of a convent and two fashionable colleges for women.

A garden of four acres originally surrounded the house, but the beautiful plantings and sculptures were destroyed in 1947. At the present time efforts are being made to restore the gardens.

The house has been restored to the period when it was occupied by the Hamptons and Prestons. Most of the furnishings currently displayed originally belonged to the family.

The men's sitting room has deep rose-colored walls, ornate white woodwork, and a beautiful marble mantelpiece carved in Italy by Hiram Powers, a noted American sculptor. The bedrooms have off-white walls with deep ivory-colored woodwork. The entryway and dining room have white walls with Williamsburg Blue carved woodwork. A beautiful spiral staircase leads to the two upper levels. The house is open to the public.

THE ROBERT MILLS HOUSE

1616 Blanding Street

Robert Mills designed this brick mansion for Ainsley Hall who died before the home was completed in 1823. It is situated on a lot that covers an entire city block in downtown Columbia. Its importance is primarily because of the architect. Mills, a native South Carolinian who studied under Hoban and Latrobe, was the first American-trained federal architect. He served under seven presidents. Mills designed the Washington Monument and was responsible in large measure for the classical style of federal buildings. Among buildings that he has designed are churches, monuments, bridges, government buildings (many county courthouses in his native state), and residences.

Columbia Theological Seminary occupied the building for many years. Woodrow Wilson's father was one of the professors who taught in this facility. Winthrop College was founded in this building in 1886.

Although the main entrance faces north, the rear entrance is just as attractive. The home is on a raised brick arcaded basement. The front has an Ionic temple portico with four huge columns, while the rear entrance has a seven-bay arched porch. The two windows on the lower level are set in recessed brick arches. On the south side there are three-part Venetian windows on both floors.

Twin drawing rooms off the central hall have curved ends. The hall is almost twice as long as it is wide and ends in a semicircular wall. There are also double parlors. In order to make the rooms symmetrical, one of the doors is false. Furnishings are American empire or Regency. This is one of the most elegant homes in the state.

It is operated as a house museum and is open to the public.

MANN-SIMONS COTTAGE (MUSEUM OF AFRICAN AMERICAN CULTURE)

1403 Richland Street

The exact date of the building of this cottage is not known. However, it has been established that Celia Mann, a Charleston slave who had bought her freedom, purchased the house in 1850. It is said that she walked from Charleston to Columbia.

Mann was born in 1799 and was an uneducated midwife who had purchased over two thousand dollars worth of real estate before she died in 1867. This was a remarkable feat for an ex-slave with four daughters. The First Calvary Baptist Church was organized in the basement of the cottage, and Mann was an active member until her death. Today the family Bible, the center of the lives of the members of this family, lies on a table in the parlor.

Agnes Jackson Simons, the oldest daughter, inherited the cottage at her mother's death. Simons lived most of her life in this house. Her husband, Bill Simons, was a prominent local musician. Their son, Charles, inherited the cottage, and the Mann-Simons family lived there until 1960. Bernice Conners, a member of the family, owned the house for ten years, after which it was sold to the Columbia Housing Authority. In 1974 it was deeded to the Historic Preservation Commission.

The main floor contains furnishings and artifacts that belonged to the family. It serves as a museum giving evidence of the manner in which free blacks lived in Columbia's antebellum period. The flooring in the parlor and other rooms is original. The molding is dropped about twelve inches from the ceiling, and that space is painted the same white color as the ceiling. The walls in the parlor are a warm grey. Lace panel curtains cover the windows, and a lovely braided circular rug covers a wide area of each room.

Dropped molding is also used in the bedroom, the walls of which are pale yellow. One small room contains a single iron bed and the tools of a midwife. Downstairs there is a gift shop and black artists' arts and crafts.

Sumter County/ Stateburg

Stateburg was founded by Gen. Thomas Sumter in 1783, and he named it "Statesborough" in the hope that it would be chosen as the capital of the state. As a matter of fact, when the decision was made in 1786, his proposition lost by just a few votes. Columbia was chosen because it was in the exact geographic center of the state. Stateburg was the center of much fighting during the Revolutionary War; General Sumter's home was destroyed. Generals Cornwallis and Greene occupied the very historic Borough House during the war. From 1783 to 1800 it was the county seat of Clarendon County.

There are several beautiful plantation homes in this area. Among those are the Borough House, the Governor Miller House, Dixie Hall, Millvale, and Marston.

The Episcopal Church of the Holy Cross was constructed of pisé de terre (rammed or packed earth) in 1850 and is located about one-half mile from the Sumter Highway on Highway 261. High Hills Baptist Church is another historic church in the area. It was organized in 1770, and the building was constructed in 1803 in the Greek Revival style. Richard Furman, the founder of Furman University, was its first pastor. As a seminary, the school was located in Stateburg from 1828 to 1835.

ELIZABETH WHITE HOUSE

412 North Main Street

John Independence Miller built two identical houses in 1850. The Elizabeth White House is the only one remaining. It is also referred to as the Anthony White House.

This house became the property of Hamilton Gillard Witherspoon of the Coldstream Plantation. It was used primarily as a summer home. Witherspoon gave the house to his daughter, Ann Reid, as a part of her dowry.

Anthony White bought the home and moved his family into it in 1878. He and his son founded Sumter's first insurance agency. He was also a member of the South Carolina House of Representatives. White's daughter, Elizabeth, inherited the house and lived there until her death in 1976. Miss White requested that the house be used by the public to promote the arts. It now houses the Sumter Gallery of Art and was listed in the National Historic Register in 1977.

Elizabeth White studied art at the Pennsylvania Academy of Fine Arts with Alfred Hutty of Charleston and with Frank Nakiveil of New York. She taught in the public schools of Sumter and in the art department of the University of South Carolina. Her postcard etchings, pastels, watercolors, and drawings are widely recognized. An oil painting entitled *Rhododendrons in Tiffany Vase* was judged "best flower painting" in the Southern States Art League Show in 1932. She was invited to work several summers in the McDowell Colony in New Hampshire.

This small white frame, one and one-half story Greek Revival-style house is quite simple in design. It is almost perfectly symmetric with the portico in the center and the windows balanced on each side. The pillars are quite large for the small portico. The entrance is through a double door which has sidelights and a beautiful transom. Dormers were added in the twentieth century.

The symmetry of the exterior is matched by that of the interior, which has a central hall and identical rooms on each side. There are back-to-back fireplaces and simple carved mantels. The upstairs is used for administrative purposes and the downstairs as a gallery, with the gallery open from 2:00 to 5:00 on Sundays and 11:00 to 5:00 Monday through Thursday from September through May. A gift shop provides some unique gift ideas, and classes and workshops are offered throughout the year.

THE BOROUGH HOUSE
Highway 261

The Borough House is the most prominent home in the village of Stateburg (Statesborough). It was formerly known as the village of Claremont. The house has sometimes been known as "Hillcrest" and "Rougemont," but has always been called the Borough House.

Constructed of pisé de terre (rammed earth), it is the oldest complex in the United States of that construction. This method was used extensively by the Babylonians and the Chinese. Walls built by this method will stand for centuries. The outside walls are covered with "crepe," a limestone and sand mixture with a little clay added. Water is added to the mixture, and it is applied to the outer walls with great force using a broom. On top of this is a pebble dash wash which makes the walls impervious to rain. The roof just sits on the rafters on top of the walls with no ridge poles. The earliest roof was of hand-hewn cypress shingles, but the entire roof was replaced with copper in 1973. The hand-hewn beams are approximately fifty feet long. Both the beams and the lathes are pegged and nailed with hand-forged nails.

The land on which the house was built was granted to William Hilton in 1758. A later owner, Thomas Hooper, was the brother of William Hooper, one of the signers of the Declaration of Independence. The earliest building was likely a tavern. A sketch of the house dated 1809 shows a front porch with wings on each side of the center room, but in 1821 these wings were replaced with pise de terre by William Wallace Anderson, a graduate of the University of Pennsylvania. He arrived in Stateburg in 1810 from Rockville, Maryland to practice medicine. In 1818 he married Mary Jane McKenzie, a niece of Mrs. Hooper. Dr. Anderson made some alterations in the house, such as adding the back portico with two bedrooms upstairs and a second-story porch on the front.

The outside walls are a soft peach color. It is one of the most impressive houses in the state. The main house is Greek Revival style of two stories with columns across the front porches; there is also a columned portico on the back. The library has columns on all four sides, and the doctor's office has a temple front with four columns. Each of these is from the heart of a single pine tree. The Loom House still contains the original looms used by the slaves for weaving cloth. There is a cotton gin of early vintage and one slave cabin remains. The other buildings contain original cooking utensils, milk churns, and pans.

The history of this house is certainly interesting and colorful. Lord Cornwallis and Gen. Nathanael Greene were reputed to have occupied the home during the Revolutionary War. There is a spring at the foot of Borough Hill still referred to as "Greene's Spring." The general's officers took red-hot pokers and branded *C A* (Confederate Army) on the panels of the downstairs doors.

Dr. Anderson and his wife inherited the house at the death of Mrs. Hooper. This outstanding physician performed the first successful surgery for cancer of the jawbone right here in the Borough House in 1829.

Borough House has been occupied by the same family for nine generations. It was placed in the National Historic Register in 1972. It is located on Highway 261 about thirteen miles west of Sumter, and is not open to the public.

Just after the turn onto Highway 261, The Church of the Holy Cross is located on the right. It is constructed of pisé de terre with walls over forty feet in height. Dr. Anderson influenced the church leadership to choose this type of construction in 1852.

GOVERNOR MILLER HOUSE

Highway 261

The Miller House is a two-story white frame building located in a grove of towering trees and set well back from the highway. It stands on a four- to five-acre plot in the southwest corner of the fork where the King's Highway (Route 261) and the Old Garner's Ferry Road meet. The earliest known records indicate that Stephen D. Miller moved into the home with his family in 1810, but there is some evidence to support an earlier date for its completion.

Governor Miller lived in the house eighteen years. He was an alumnus of South Carolina College (University of South Carolina), having graduated in 1808. Subsequently, he studied law in the office of John Richardson of Sumter and was admitted to the bar in 1811. He was a member of the South Carolina House of Representatives from 1817 to 1819 and served as a state senator from 1822 to 1828. Miller was governor from 1828 to 1830 and in 1831 was elected to the United States Senate. His law office was located in the little building that remains on the property.

The Ellison family, a free black family, bought the house in 1838. For more than fifty years the Ellisons manufactured the standard cotton gin used in the South. Their business was known as the Ellison Cotton Gin Company. The Ellisons owned the property until 1922, when it was sold to Mary Virginia Sanders White. It later became a part of the Borough Plantation.

Martha Wallace White purchased the house from the Borough Plantation early in 1964. A contract for restoration was let to the Pine Tree Building Company with Henry T. Boykin II as consultant. Part of the evidence for the determination of the age of this house may have been destroyed at the time of this restoration. At this time there was some modernization with the addition of bathrooms and other conveniences.

This charming house has four rooms downstairs and upstairs with a narrow hallway dividing both floors. The windows are nine over nine and have old glass in them. A kitchen wing was added at a later date. It was four to six inches higher than the lower floor and was leveled during the restoration. There are four chimneys on the main section, each with different brickwork. The two rear chimneys appear to be the older ones. The siding is of two widths separated by a strip. Wide heart-pine boards were used for the paneling. No two mantels are alike. One set of the beams in the attic extends forty feet front to back and is of hand-hewn heart pine. This set is attached to another set that is also hand-hewn heart pine and extends only to the wall between the front and back rooms. The hinges on the doors range from very old strap-type to Holy Land and Self-rising. The doors are either plain boards or cross and Bible design. The nails that were used in the house were made before 1800.

Still standing are three original outbuildings which were used as a smokehouse, carriage house, and office. The mantel in the office is from the Empire Period.

DIXIE HALL

Highway 261

In 1735 William Sanders built Dixie Hall, which is probably the oldest home in the vicinity. For a number of years it was the only house in the area except for Indian homes. The home rests on a high brick basement which contains three storage rooms. The two upper levels are white frame with a two-story porch on the front. The windows are all nine over nine flanked by dark plantation shutters. A wide central hall extends from the front to the back with two large rooms on each side. This is the floor plan for both levels. The first floor contains a parlor, master bedroom, formal dining room, and library, with connecting doors between the rooms. There is attractive woodwork on the doors, windows, and paneled wainscoting in each of these rooms. Each room has a fireplace, and no two mantels are alike. Ceilings in the downstairs rooms are fourteen feet high. On the upper level are four large bedrooms, with chair rails in three and paneled wainscoting in the other. Each room has a fireplace, and each mantel is unique. The ceilings upstairs are twelve feet high. Above the turn of the stairway at the back of the hall is a window to light the way.

The entrance is a beautifully detailed door with sidelights, a transom, and Doric pilasters at each side. The crown of the pilasters is repeated at the top of the interior doors on the first floor. The upstairs door to the porch is a smaller version of those downstairs.

There is now a family room and a modern kitchen at the rear of the home. Records do not indicate when this addition was made.

A cannonball was found on the hearth in one room. It had been shot into the house when General Potter raided these homes in 1865.

The house is in the process of being restored by the owner. Dixie Hall is located on the left, nine miles from the junction of the Sumter Highway and Highway 261.

MILLVALE

Ellarbe Mill Road

An iron archway frames the entrance to Millvale on Ellarbe Mill Road. Red-painted frame buildings are on each side of the entrance drive. Ellarbe Mill has operated since the early nineteenth century, and the dam on the creek was built before 1790.

This Victorian house with its white "gingerbread" and "dripping lace" is reflected in the mill pond and creates a very picturesque scene. In 1890, William Crawford Sanders Ellarbe built this home with its large rooms and two-story verandahs. It is located about halfway between Sumter and Camden in an area made up of highly valued farmland. Three-fourths of the plantations were built on one side of Rafting Creek and Ellarbe's Mill Pond. On the other side of the creek the land rises abruptly about one hundred feet and forms the "High Hills of Santee." (Marston and Edgehill plantations are located in that area.) It was favored as a resort area among the people from lower South Carolina.

When the Union troops were threatening to burn the mill, a man secured the owner's masonic apron and held it up. The Union commander, a mason, spared the building.

Millvale suffered extensive damage from the winds and rain of Hurricane Hugo. After all the damage has been repaired it is not known at this writing whether or not the mill and the attendant buildings will be reopened.

To reach Millvale from Columbia turn left off of the Sumter Highway onto Highway 261. Drive eight miles to the Rafting Creek School and turn right onto Ellarbe Mill Road. The entrance to Millvale is approximately one mile from that point. The road is well marked.

MARSTON

2280 Racoon Road

Located on one of the High Hills of Santee is Marston, a stately plantation home built by Patrick Henry Nelson in the 1800s. One of the early owners was S. Oliver Plowdens, but the most notable was Col. John J. Dargen, a teacher, historian, and entrepreneur who authored the book entitled *School History of South Carolina.* A school that he built in a nearby plantation home was the forerunner of rural schools in the state. He was a great admirer of Gen. Thomas Sumter and named the school in his honor. He also was very influential in the project to mark General Sumter's grave.

Fourteen huge white columns outline the wide piazzas that circle the white stucco house on four sides. The design is a modified classical, and the plan is very simple: a central hall with two rooms on each side on both floors. There was a parlor on each level. The halls are twenty feet wide and the ceilings in all the rooms are thirteen feet high. Originally, there were steps that went up the center of the south side of the house to the second level of the piazza. There are plans to replace these steps. The entrances on both levels are very lovely double doors with sidelights and transoms. The carriage drive circles to this side of the house; at the present time the drive approach is to the rear. The outside walls are eleven inches thick creating a very comfortable environment. The original tin roof had to be replaced after Hurricane Hugo. Estimated damage to the house was two hundred thousand dollars. The upstairs plastered ceilings suffered so much damage that they had to be replaced. The present owners are in the process of restoring the home to its original glory.

To reach the mansion traveling from Columbia, turn off the Sumter Highway onto Highway 261. Two miles from this intersection turn right on Racoon Road. About two or three miles down Racoon Road there is a water tank which is a prominent landmark. Take the dirt road on the left just before reaching the water tank.

Camden

Camden was named in 1730 to honor Charles Pratt, Earl of Camden. It was settled by a few English families who were Irish Quakers. A Cattawba Indian chief, King Haigler, befriended the settlers and came to their aid when war broke out with the other Indians.

During the Revolutionary War, General Cornwallis captured Camden and made it the chief British garrison of the state. It was recaptured by the American forces in 1781, but before they retreated the British burned most of the city.

George Washington and the Marquis de LaFayette are among the important people who have visited here. Bernard Baruch was born in one of the old homes. Another has been in the family of William F. Buckley for years. John Buckley, noted author, still maintains a studio on the grounds of one of the historic homes.

Dr. George Todd, a relative of Mary Todd Lincoln, is buried in the Old Quaker Burying Ground. During the War Between the States he was a surgeon in the hospital that was set up in Camden to care for the wounded.

Camden is noted for the "Carolina Cup," a steeplechase race. This beautiful city, with its numerous old homes, is well prepared for visitors. There are markers in front of the historically significant homes. The personnel at the Camden Archives and Museum as well as the Visitor's Center are most gracious to those seeking information. A Candlelight Tour and a Spring Tour feature a number of homes each year. Contact the Visitor's Center for the dates.

Bed and breakfast inns are in several old homes. Camden is located east of Columbia on Interstate Highway 20.

OLD METHODIST PARSONAGE (WIMBERLY HALL)

314 Hampton Park

Wimberly Hall was deeded to the trustees of Lyttleton Street United Methodist Church in September 1852 by Sarah Ciples and Amelia Haile. The gift included some furnishings and some slaves. According to archival records they also gave some stock in the Bank of Camden to provide money for the upkeep of the house and care for the slave families. Church records indicate that the home was built before August 1852. A tribute was adopted in church conference in 1880 that mentioned the death of Sister Amelia Haile. Sarah Ciples was not mentioned at that time. In a conference report in 1883, note is made that the parsonage was being "fitted up" and repaired.

The home continued to be used as a parsonage until the 1950s. When Dr. Charles Wimberly became pastor in 1932, he expressed a desire to use the basement for church growth. Some of the basement was converted to Sunday School space, and a kitchen was installed for church use. The name of the home became Wimberly Hall in his honor. It is now being used for child care.

Square Doric columns rise from the ground and support the shed roof of the one-tiered portico. The white frame two-story house rests on a full basement and has a lovely double staircase that extends to the main floor. The windows are six over six. The doors on the basement level and the first floor have sidelights and transoms, and the balustrade on the portico is very lovely with its turned balusters interspersed with square posts.

WASHINGTON HOUSE

1413 Mill Street

The house is named in honor of George Washington, who was entertained here when he visited Camden on May 25, 1791. He was on a tour of the Southern states. After many speeches the citizens of Camden entertained with a reception and an elaborate banquet.

Col. John Chestnut built the house and it was originally on the corner of South Fair and King streets. It was moved to this location in the early 1900s by Henry Savage. Elise Long owned the home for many years and then left it to her daughter, Julia Long Knapp. Later it was purchased by the John Whitakers.

Four square posts support the flat roof, which is crowned with a delicate latticework balustrade. The white frame, two-story home has dark shutters on each side of the nine-over-nine windows. The front entrance is impressive with its intricate sidelights and sunburst transom.

Camden sponsors a Spring Tour and a Candlelight Tour during the Christmas season. Contact the Camden Visitor's Center for information.

ABERDEEN (MATHIS HOUSE)

1409 Broad Street

Samuel Mathis is believed to be the first white baby born in Camden. In 1805 he purchased the property on which this house stands from his brother-in-law, Joseph Kershaw, in an extensive land deal. Because of financial problems, Kershaw was selling much of his property.

Mathis built his home of pine in the early 1800s. There have been changes in the intervening years. Above a full basement, four rooms were used for living quarters. Later the kitchen was attached to the back of the house and porches were added. The decorative bargeboard on the gables and the jigsaw trim were probably added in the late nineteenth century. This one-story frame house has twelve-foot ceilings. Under the gables are narrow double windows with a pair of small triangular pediments. The front entrance has sidelights and a triangular transom that has ogee-shaped arched woodwork. The house is very lovely. The view of the back and side of the house is as nice as the front.

Although he was a sixteen-year-old, Quaker Mathis joined the Patriot Army when the Revolutionary War began. He was captured by the British in Charleston in 1780. After the war he opened a store in Camden and also practiced law. He was involved in some notable legal cases. Dr. Leslie Zemp bought the home from Mathis. In 1860 Zemp sold it to I. W. R. Blair. Because of heavy debts, Blair sold it back to Zemp in 1872, and Zemp sold it to Valentine Smith Jordan that same year. Later owners were Annie McDowell, H. G. Garrison, T. R. Team, Col. W. A. Metts, and Jack Brantley.

Aberdeen is a bed and breakfast inn.

JOSEPH KERSHAW HOUSE (DELOACH HOUSE)

1305 Lyttleton Street

The date of the construction of this house is not known. It is thought to have been part of the Joshua Reynolds House on Broad Street and was moved to this location in 1842. Joseph Kershaw, of Yorkshire, England, owned the land on which it now stands. He went to the area called "Pine Tree Hill" as a merchant in 1758, and soon owned most of the area now known as Camden, becoming a very wealthy man. Kershaw's service in the Revolutionary War resulted in much suffering and exile as a prisoner of war. He lost much of his property. His family was forced to leave the home because it was confiscated by Cornwallis to be used for British Headquarters. After the war he returned to Camden. When the county was formed in 1791, it was named Kershaw County in honor of his war efforts. After his death his brother-in-law, Samuel Mathis, bought the house. In 1850 Joseph Brevard Kershaw, the grandson of the original Kershaw, acquired the property, and it has remained in the family since that date. The young Kershaw attained the rank of general of the army during the War Between the States and became quite famous.

During the war the family hid the silver in the well. After the war, when the family was having great financial difficulties, the silver was sent north to be auctioned one piece at a time. A friend learned of this, quietly purchased the silver, and returned it to Mrs. Kershaw.

Joseph Kershaw probably extended each side of the two-story white frame house after it was moved. The front porch that stretches across the length of the first floor and the smaller second-floor porch were added at a later date. An unusual feature is that the six windows of the first floor were designed in such a way that when the window is raised the wall area below it could swing out and create a doorway. The windowpanes are handblown and names etched on the glass record the occupants. The house was built of pine with ceilings of ten feet on the first level and fourteen feet on the second. The floors are wide polished pine boards.

The home is privately owned. Contact the Camden Visitor's Center for possible tours.

MARTHA MCINTOSH HOME
Society Hill

Society Hill is a very small town with a "very big history." The Welsh Neck Baptist Church was organized in 1738 and is the second oldest Baptist church in South Carolina.

James Hart McIntosh, a wealthy merchant and planter, built this home in 1840. Timbers in the attic that extend the length of the house give evidence of being put together with pegs. It is a white frame, two-story home on a raised basement. Originally the one-story verandah wrapped around each end of the house. Later, one end was enclosed to accommodate a study.

This was the home of David Gregg McIntosh, a captain of the Pee Dee Light Artillery during the War Between the States. He was later an attorney in Baltimore, Maryland. Martha McIntosh, another member of the family, is very important in Baptist history. She was the first president of Woman's Missionary Union, an auxiliary to the Southern Baptist Convention.

This is a private home.

REFERENCES

Architecture of the Old South—South Carolina by Mills Lane.

Archival records from the cities of Charleston, Columbia, Camden, Conway, Sumter, and Pendleton

Backward Glances Vol. I and II published by Colleton Artists' Guild.

George Washington Guide to Waccamaw Neck and Georgetown by Shanon Carlisle.

A Goodly Heritage by Anne P. Collins.

Greenwood County by Greenwood Artist Guild.

Greenwood County Sketches by Margaret Watson.

A Guide to Historic Beaufort published by Historic Beaufort Foundation.

Historic Pendleton published by Pendleton District Historic Commission.

Illustrated Dictionary of Historic Architecture by Cyril M. Harris.

Laurens County Sketchbook by Julian Stevenson Bolick.

Plantation Heritage by Kenneth and Blanche Marsh.

62 Famous Houses of Charleston published by the *Post-Courier*

The Villa, Saga of Five Families by Julia Chiles Lovell.

INDEX